In the SHADOW of the GODS

The Memoirs of a Led Zeppelin Tribute Singer

Written By Jean Violet and Aaron Joy

Copyright © 2021 by Jean Violet & Aaron Joy
All rights reserved
First Edition

Published by Roman Midnight Music.
Printing and distribution by Lulu Press.
Worldwide printing and distribution by Ingram Press.

ISBN: 978-1-716-16719-5

Contact the authors directly for all comments, sales inquires:
aronmatyas@hotmail.com
P.O. Box 15382, Portland, Maine 04112 USA

Visit Kashmir at kashmirrocks.com

Kashmir's booking through Blue Raven Artists
blueravenartists.com

DEDICATED TO:

Our rocks of support

Marilyn
&
Jamie

1
CANDY STORE ROCK

The fact that a young band is influenced by us is not bad, and in fact, is downright natural. Every musician learns their craft from other players. That's the way it's always been, and that's the only way it really should be.
~ Robert Plant

My first singing gig didn't pay, wasn't glamorous, didn't get me signed to any labels, and it may not even have been that good of quality in hindsight, but it verified to me that I loved singing and performing. In my early teens I spent a few months regularly calling in to a local Rochester radio station's talent hour with DJ Paul Barsky to sing Beatles songs over the air. DJ Barsky would go on to host a show on one of the first satellite radio subscription services, so at age 13 I was crying about how you can't buy me love to a future respected radio name.

Eventually my brother joined me for those Lennon-McCartney harmonies. Girls would call in to the show raving about us after our performances. I had a girlfriend at the time, but my brother didn't, so he would go out and meet some of the girls. We loved the Beatles. When I discovered the Beatles I just opened up musically. My world was forever changed.

Music actually runs in my family. My brother would go on to sing in the hard rock band Pistol Dawn playing the New York City clubs, not to be confused with the band of the same name that released the album <u>Conversation Piece</u>. While my nephew, Carson Schaller, plays bass in the nu-metal trio Deviate The Plan, who did an album with one of Megadeth's engineers. Going back in time my father's family were well-known musicians from Germany. My great-uncle played in John Phillip Sousa's band. I believe he played clarinet and other reed instruments. While my grandfather was a drummer in the New Jersey/New York City circuit.

My family became born again Christians when I was about thirteen years old, so there were restrictions when it came to how rock'n'roll fit into my life. They've seen me perform and have listened to the music I've made, but I've had some uncomfortable debates with my mom over Led Zeppelin and the questionable reputations of other rock bands. My father was a plumber who had his own business. He worked hard to support his wife and five kids, so even if they had restrictions on us, at least in the long run they supported my musical endeavors.

Yet, if someone had told my young Beatles loving self that decades later I would be fronting a Led Zeppelin tribute band for over two decades I would have been shocked and then laughed. I was not in the least a Zeppelin fan growing up. That was my older sister's favorite band. They were good, but I didn't appreciate them. They also weren't as good as the bands I loved at that time.

My young ears gravitated to the cutting edge New Wave scene that was plastered all over the revolutionary new medium of MTV. I was into the Psychedelic Furs, Devo, U2, Split Enz, INXS, the Cult and other such bands, though I also liked things like AC/DC, Judas Priest and Elvis Costello. I was fascinated by interesting and visual frontmen who did more than just sing but brought something unique to the music. I like the charisma a great frontman brings to the stage. They connect with the crowd like its a transfer of energy. I'm big into people and moving energy between them. I would study these frontmen. I wanted to be one of them. I wanted to move energy around with a crowd of strangers all high on the music and a band feeding it. I wanted to be more than just a singer, but also a conductor of energy.

I would eventually graduate from singing Beatles songs to unsuspecting radio listeners to being in a barbershop quartet at my Christian school. At the end of my high school years I joined a metal band trying to be Rob Halford of Judas Priest. I hooked up with the guys in music class and we started jamming. We only played a couple shows.

After graduation I decided to go to the Art Institute of Pittsburgh. I graduated with an Associates in Visual Communications with a plan to go into advertising and commercial art. I've never given much thought to a career in the fine arts. I studied illustration and graphic design via all styles of art and mediums of creation, to be fully prepared for anything I might be asked to do in the commercial art world. This was when computers were just getting into play on a mass scale, so it was an exciting time to be an artist and have my palette expanded in such incredible ways.

I was really interested in fashion illustration. That was not just about cool clothing, but about a flashy lifestyle that included chasing girls, looking great, and entertaining people.

Art and music, and girls, were my passions growing up. They all intertwined and fed off each other and inspired each other. Art and music has co-existed my entire life. The New Wave music I loved obviously had a strong visual and artistic component. I really liked graphic artist Patrick Nagel who is famous for doing the cover of Duran Duran's Rio album, featuring only the bare shouldered bust of a smiling woman with simple black lines and only a few strong colors. That's not just great art, but also sets a mood for the music, creates a visual aspect to a new music-based culture, and helps sell the album and band. Advertising, fashion, emotion and and art are fused together in one simple but powerful drawing. I wanted to create art like that.

For most of my high school years I had gone to a Christian school. That was before we left Rochester and I went back to public school, and to the dark side with my short-lived metal band. The discipline of the Christian school was good and kept me out of trouble, but the art classes were the worst. I think it was a big set-back for me in my early development as an artist. I eventually made up for it, but I wish I'd had more basic art training in school. Though, I did what I could under my own initiative throughout all my school years. I remember illustrating murals for my elementary school principal and creating dinosaur books for the school library. I made posters of E.T. when the movie came out and sold them to my schoolmates, and I did silk screening like Andy Warhol popularized. I also directed little plays I'd made-up.

2

ROCK & ROLL

We seem to live our lives around computers and in front of screens. A live concert breaks you away from that and helps you share an experience with others. Live music is a celebration that goes along with creating a connective moment.
~ Ian Astbury

A girl at the Art Institute knew of a New Wave band that was looking for a singer. I auditioned and they picked me. We were called Avant Garde. Not to be confused with the Avant Garde that featured future Weezer founder Rivers Cuomo. We were trying to be Duran Duran meets Love And Rockets, which a lot of people don't remember but was formed by guys from Bauhaus. My guitar player and I looked just like the lead singer of Love And Rockets who had big spiky hair and flashy clothes. In hindsight we probably looked more like roosters to some gawkers. From the Beatles to barbershop to metal to New Wave, I was spreading my musical wings and flying with big dreams and ambitions, and doing it with visual flair.

Our set list was almost evenly split between originals and covers. I sang stuff by the Psychedelic Furs, Duran Duran, Pet Shop Boys, U2, INXS and other bands of that nature. I also wrote some real catchy pop songs. 'You're Always There' I actually wrote on the spot at my audition. It got me the gig.

We got signed to one of the best agents in Pittsburgh and played all around the region for the next two years. We had a strong following as one of the big bands of the area. This was in the days when a band could be booked numerous days a week, often as a house band at one club, while paying gigs of all shapes and sizes were plentiful. People of all ages went out to hear live music Wednesday through Saturday. They don't do that today. The scene is completely different now for both audiences and bands. People might go find a DJ to dance to or head to a quiet bar for drinks, but they don't see live music as regularly nor take a chance on unknown bands as much. Going to a bar was also a way to socialize and meet other musicians, something that today happens more and more over the internet.

Avant Garde often played four days a week, sometimes with three sets a night, and we would make like $1200 a week. For a 21 year old I was in musical heaven. Let alone, playing so much one hones their craft really fast and gets really tight with fellow bandmates. Bands don't have an opportunity to do this anymore when they are starting out. Today a young band might perform once or twice a month, if not less than that, with a single 30 minute set, while the role of a house band is often taken up by DJ's.

At the same time, during the day I was doing different art jobs for various lengths of time. I did some freelance newspaper stuff and illustrations for a Realtor. I also worked, though it sounds almost cliched, in a clothing store and a record store. These were really wild days and I was right in the middle of that flashy fashionable world I loved with art and music every where I turned.

A high point for Avant Garde was opening for the Smithereens at a college in Akron, Ohio. They made it big when a song from their debut album landed on TV's Miami Vice. This was my first experience opening for a nationally known band. I remember they took forever at soundcheck.

We would play anywhere and for anyone who would listen. Though, our agent took this to heart a little bit too much for our liking at times. He booked us a gig at a co-ed detention center for kids. Or, so we thought. It was really a men's minimum security prison. Here I was dressed in eye liner, spiky hair, colorful clothing and there's this inmate telling everyone what he is going to do to me as we set up our gear. We played at one end of a baseball field to 500 guys. I'm not sure if they were New Wave fans, but at the end the only thing we could say to our manager was, "What the hell was that?" To which we were told, "A job's a job."

There was another time we played Carnegie Mellon University during their Rush Week. We were in the basement of a frat house which was set-up like a night club. We had multiple guitars, drums, keyboards, amps, cables, and the whole nine yards that every band hauls around with them. When we were done we turned on the lights to unplug and pack up. One of the frat boys turned off the lights saying, "You're done. You need to leave." We were leaving, but we needed to see our stuff. We turned the lights back on. Then they turned them off again. I don't know what they were thinking, but they weren't joking as this went on for thirty minutes. The lights would go on and off while they got increasingly mad and we kept pleading for light. They obviously didn't realize that if they left the lights on we'd be out of there sooner, as we wanted to get out of their hair as fast as they wanted us out of it. It was reaching confrontation stage. One of my guys even tried to splice into their electrical system to keep the lights on.

Suddenly, the fire alarm was pulled. I don't know who did it, us or them, or if it was an accident or deliberate, but it was the distraction we needed before they decided to beat the hell out of us. Under its blare we were no longer important and could quickly finish packing. As we were leaving the fire department showed up wondering who did that, since there was no fire. "I don't know, we just want to get out of here," we pleaded.

We eventually performed at CBGB's a couple times to get noticed by industry representatives and in turn signed to a label. To come to New York City to perform at the legendary rock club was a big dream come true for me and a huge deal for the band. This was the dirtiest club around, bringing the definition of dive bar to a new low level, but it also was where every band went to showcase for label representatives and its influence on the New York music scene was nothing less than iconic. Since opening in 1973, playing at CBGB's was nearly a rite of passage so many bands dreamed of. After it closed in 2006 bands would then wish they had played there. This was an important stepping stone on our career path. It was also just a lot of fun. I was born in the city, but left as a child so it was a new and unfamiliar adventure hanging out in the city.

Following both gigs, nothing happened. I can't remember if any label people were there. I don't think there was. Things were changing and hair metal was coming to dominate. We had the big hair, but not the right sound. Our time had passed. New Wave bands didn't have the customer draw or relevancy anymore. Labels and clubs didn't want bands playing our style of music. Gigs were slowly becoming harder to find, or not as lucrative. We ended up splitting not long after. CBGB's ended up being a way to go out on a high, than to gain traction.

Yet, on some level, none of us were surprised how nothing happened for the band. We saw the change in music and were enjoying the new bands and new sounds as much as anyone. We'd also gone through a few members over the years, so we were naturally discovering new and different directions to grow alongside the changing national music scene.

We were at a crossroads. We were debating our future musical direction, including a desire to start playing hard rock. We also didn't know if we wanted to keep playing covers or focus more on our originals to the eventual exclusion of covers. It took originals to get a record deal, which is something myself, my bassist and drummer wanted. The three of us nearly lusted after a record deal. Our guitarist worked a record store and enjoyed his day job and gigging on the side for fun and extra money. We were being drawn to New York City and doing whatever we could to get a deal, but the guitarist didn't really want to do that. This conflict routinely came up between us and was only exasperated by the decline in New Wave's popularity and commercial viability. The lack of label interest following the CBGB's gigs didn't destroy us, as if we hadn't collapsed then we likely would have at some point in the near future. In the least, we would have gone through more membership changes and morphed into a new band with a non-New Wave sound.

Yet, the collapse of Avant Garde was just a minor hurdle. I had places to go and songs to write and sing. I was just getting started. I was young, hungry and ready to conquer the musical world.

3

DANCING DAYS

I've been a music fan and a fan of all things that are interesting and occasionally unique so I'm always a member of the audience and an entertainer really.
~ Robert Plant

I wanted to be this rock star. This guy that is on MTV. That is on the radio.

During the day I was drawing art on a desk to pay my expenses, while at night I was creating living art on stage for more money. I loved it all, except that the night gig was the unquestionable priority for my ambitious young self.

It was such a priority that I passed on a potentially lucrative job doing fashion illustration for an art agency right out of college. It was at graduation. I had my portfolio at a fair for perspective employment. This woman from an agency in Buffalo really liked my stuff and essentially was offering me a job on the spot. It would undoubtedly get my foot in the door, yet my mind was elsewhere. Avant Garde had a gig that night. I was going right from the college to the gig, so I was dressed in my stage clothes as I had little time to waste. I had a long white coat, magenta belt, red shoes, white pants, tie, and my hair was blasting. Of course, I passed on the job. That clearly shows where my head was in those early days.

I was solely focused on what was next for my music. I was going to make my dreams come true. Moving to the Big Apple was the obvious next step to be near influential people and be part of a vibrant music scene.

After the dissolution of Avant Garde my drummer Mark and my bassist Kurt Foltz moved to New York City. I went down to Florida to stay with my parents and make some money. In a couple months I would join them in the big city ready to rock again.

The three of us formed Black Bullet to play the hard rock we were hearing on the radio. It would eventually morph into Naked City.

The line-up was rounded out by a guitarist named Brian Kreis and a guitarist from Rocket Angel named Michael Angelo. My brother also came up from Florida and did backing vocals on some of our first shows at the Limelight, though from the side of the stage.

We were highly influenced by Guns N' Roses and the Cult, though the <u>East Coast Rocker</u> magazine, today <u>The Aquarian Weekly</u>, would call us a New York version of L.A. Guns. Some might also compare us to '80's Black Sabbath music-wise, given our heavy sound alongside my mystical lyrics. My guitarist even wore a cross necklace like Sabbath guitarist Tony Iommi was famous for.

Yet, under the our mystical and heavy mood, the music was gritty and very much New York City sounding hard rock. I do think there's a distinctive New York sound. Its more wet, more organic, kinda tinnier, and a little bit hot. Its hard to describe, but I know it when I hear it. Its sleazy, but grittier than the more famous sleazy West Coast glam metal, such as by Mötley Crüe and Poison. I think Guns N' Roses have a bit of a New York flavor in their sound. Skin N' Bones, who we used to hang out with, is another who have that gritty sound, though they're not as well known. Circus Of Power is another that have the New York sound, with vocals like the Misfits. They were a wild band that were in the same circles as we were. I remember one show of ours when one of the Circus guys slapped the ass of my then girlfriend. She was from Venezuela. Living up to the feisty stereotype, my friend and Skin N' Bones member Jimi Bones had to calm her down. It really was a circus those days, though I don't know who had the power, if any of us.

Along with the new sound I also moved my image away from Duran Duran and deliberately copied the persona of Cult frontman Ian Astbury. The Cult was really big at the time. Everyone went nuts when they released the single 'Love Removal Machine.' I'd see all these guys in the East Village with jet black hair, pale skin, and fancy clothes trying to imitate Ian in what would later be called an early goth look.

I loved Ian's look and lyrics. It didn't hurt that girls loved it too. I always thought Ian had this really cool mystical vibe, with a touch of Jim Morrison and Robert Plant. I got to see them live for the first time when they released the Love album in 1985. He was, and still is, an amazing frontman and entertainer. Watching him was hypnotically an almost timeless experience, with this spiritual essence in the atmosphere like watching Icarus taking flight on stage. He moved that energy around on stage that I loved to see. When they performed 'Rain' it was like we were all Indians dancing around a fire. I might compare this to what people recall about Jim Morrison, who is said to have made Doors performances into events that transcended the music.

I wanted this same feeling and energy transference for Naked City. Just like Ian I dyed my hair black, plus wore jackets and vests. It was very artistic and glamorous. My bassist Kurt and I even had a pair of leather pants made by the girl who went on to make clothes for L.A. Guns and Faster Pussycat. Kurt jokes today we were trendsetters and didn't know it. We appeared on the public access TV show New York New Rock which, from 1990 to 2000, would interview and feature live performances by New York and New Jersey bands. There's a 12 minute clip surviving online of us performing. I'm in a black jacket and leather pants twirling around and jumping off stage, while my guitarist falls on the ground soloing.

Alongside Ian's look sat my mystical lyrics of vampires, magic and that sorta stuff. Lyrics like "magic starts at midnight / she'll hit you right between the eyes" or "you could get lost inside my mind". I've always found New Age, magic and mystical stuff interesting. I've even been known to howl at the stars and dance around late night fires with a drum circle pounding away. Its kinda ironic I would come to play Led Zeppelin given Jimmy Page's well known connections to the occult, including owning a mansion on the Loch Ness Lake and buying an occult focused bookstore. I believe he actually tapped into something that he was familiar with to help the band's career. Jimmy knew what he was getting into, but I believe the other members were naive and just went with the flow and from that controversies and rumors sprang.

My lyrics were also inspired by experiences that happened to me. Later I started to listen more to things going on around me for inspiration. Like somebody would say something in a conversation and I'd put it into a song. Sometimes I would come up with complimentary melodies and bring them to Brian and Mike to work out on guitar. Not counting the recorder we all learned in primary school, I've never played an instrument. I've always seen myself as a frontman and lyricist. I wrote some really cool stuff for Naked City. We had a really cool 'Miss Liberty' about the statue. It would be perfect for the social strife of the current days. 'City That Never Sleeps' is about our town, cause every New York band at some point sings about their beloved home.

These songs actually keyed into the name of the band. Kurt and I were going through tons of names. Naked City was the name of a TV crime drama about detectives in gritty Brooklyn, running from 1958 to 1963. It always concluded with a voice over saying, "There are 8 million stories in the naked city. This has been one of them." Naked City and my lyrics were going to be our stories.

I was lucky. I had a great manager in Don Hill, who also became a great friend who believed in my talent and potential. If there was anyone in my circle who had pull on higher up music industry folks it was Don. Don is iconic to many musicians as he managed and booked bands into Kenny's Castaways, the Bitter End, the Cat Club and his own unabashedly named Don Hill's. He was an important mover and shaker of the rock scene from the 70's until he died in 2011, helping many bands on their rise up the career ladder. He was a businessman and a music lover. He was also one of the nicest guys I've ever known in the business.

Don's partner was Jonathan Love, who also helped me out as a friend and businessman. The pair were going to manage bands and get label deals for them. They'd already had some success getting some label and publishing deals, and Naked City were in line waiting for our turn. Jonathan's father owned a publishing company, so it was also a family business. I remember he had a sign on his office wall that said, "In order to know where you're going you always have to remember where you've been." That had a huge influence on me at a point when I was discovering the highs and lows of the music world. That's the way one has to be in this business, so I've learned.

There was a guy who helped Don and Jonathan out who was a lawyer and worked for Geffen Records, which was representing a whose who from Cher and Elton John to

Whitesnake and Nirvana. I remember he once said to me, "Its all about kissing ass. At first, you're going to kiss everyone's ass. Then when you make it they're going to kiss your ass." I was pretty lucky to have such a power trio in my corner helping me steer my career, let alone my personal growth. I took it all in as the eager student I was.

To help me grow Don got me my first formal voice training at this time. He got me a class with Don Lawrence at his Upper East Side studio. He is a choir director who specializes in classical opera techniques, but became famous by making traditional Italian vocal opera techniques work for rock singers like Sebastian Bach, Bono, Lady Gaga, Billy Joel, Mick Jagger and countless others. He taught me this technique that's not just about singing but also thinking about the whole vocal process. He taught me to picture the voice as right behind the head. He's really intense, but he's also really good at what he did. The lessons I still use decades later and recommend to other singers.

Naked City lasted a couple years and became a hot ticket. That was a really wild experience and great time. I was in my mid-20's and partying and playing like every young wannabe rock star. There was a lot of stuff going on at that time that was exciting. We all did crazy stuff we might not do today or in hindsight, honestly. For example, there was an MTV VJ named Steve Isaacs who was also into the Cult. We both fashioned our image in the style of Ian Astbury, and I was often told Steve and I looked alike. There was an event happening at Webster's Hall in Manhattan. I went over and folks thought I was Steve. I just played it, as a V.I.P. pass was put into my hand for a private party in a room upstairs. I got to meet Duran Duran. Then the real Steve showed up, and we're looking at each other. "Hey, Steve, I'm you!" I ran outside before much more was said.

I remember one time we were playing at Don Hill's. We were the last band, preceded by Tommy & The Love Tribe and another band. The opening band was going long, so one of the Love Tribe pulled the plug on their P.A.. That same guy was a practical joker who would stand outside the door and charge an entry fee, which customers would then be legitimately asked for again once they went through the door. Today craziness like this would likely bring the police and maybe lawyers. The '80's and

'90's were different times for bands in a music scene and culture that doesn't exist anymore.

On top of having fun, everyone was always keeping their eyes open for anything that might fall across their path that would take them to the next level. Everyone seemed to have multiple bands they were in, as none of us ever knew where something might lead. Though, I was a minority as I put my total focus on Naked City. I always have given the project I'm on my undivided attention. I have never been one of those mercenaries who play in fifteen bands never quite committed and always struggling with scheduling and ethical conflicts. Drummers were always considered the biggest mercenaries. Everybody was trying to steal the five good drummers that played with every band.

We all lived music all day every day. We were the music, whatever the music was. One thing that stands out in my mind about life in Pittsburgh and New York City in the '80's and '90's is the cultural unity. I had friends that were black, white, of every nationality one can think of, rich and poor. We were all playing music together and hanging out together. Everybody got along. Everybody was friends. Everybody was playing in each other's bands or supporting each other's bands. We were all living the music like that was the most important thing in the world, with music tearing down all the boundaries between us. We loved it all and we all shared with each other our latest discoveries whatever they may be. We were all listening to Run-D.M.C. and Depeche Mode and everything in between.

Today I feel like there is something that has come between all of us pushing us apart socially. In my youth everybody was listening to the same type of music, but today there's a sense of possession and tribal division. There's this feeling that some people can't listen to a certain type of music because they don't belong to a certain group or culture or age bracket. I don't feel the unity is there anymore. Its almost like in the last few decades somebody figured out a way to divide us for some unknown grand scheme, but its really not to our benefit. We had social strife back in the day, no doubt, but something was different about the music scene at least. Or, to put it another way, we all were wearing wild clothes with wild hair and looking like we were a real live <u>Back To The Future</u>. Today, older and wiser, we all, whatever ethnicity we are, equally cringe when looking back at the photos, while wishing we had those young bodies. In twenty years from now will we be able to look back on the present day in the same way? I don't know.

Between Naked City and Avant Garde I had some of the wildest gigs of my career. Right out the door, when we were still Black Bullet, we were lost in crazy times, deliberately or not. Avant Garde had regularly played at the Pittsburgh's Someplace Else club. After we regrouped in New York we got a gig there, except instead of promoting us as Black Bullet the venue owner advertised it as an Avant Garde reunion. We didn't know this, and even if we did there was no intention of a reunion and playing the old songs. We were happy with our new heavy sound and look.

I was really nervous, being a home turf gig. A friend at the club had some blood pressure medicine and gave me some to calm my nerves. It came with his stern warning not to drink. Did I listen?

The show was sold out. Except, it was sold out for Avant Garde not Black Bullet. By the time the gig started I was flying off the medicine and alcohol mix I'd put in my system. After a song I boldly declared we were Black Bullet and if the audience didn't like it there was a couple ungraceful things that they could do. One of the more graceful options was taken, as about 85 percent of the audience walked out. We kept playing, but I didn't remember much after that. The owner started freaking out and got really upset at us. He also owned a hotel where he put us up, but was ready to kick us out on the street for the night. I embarrassingly worked everything out with him, but that was not one of my better performances. On the other hand, setting aside my opening declaration, it might have been a good performance, given I can't remember a thing about it. It certainly wasn't the performance anyone wanted.

Naked City performed for a handful of private parties for the Hell's Angels. They have a little club tucked away on an unassuming residential street in lower Manhattan. We did that kinda as a favor to them, as in return they would protect us at our shows elsewhere. I don't know if we always needed protection, but it was nice to not worry as drunken altercations did occasionally flash up putting us and others at physical risk. I wound up designing t-shirts for them. I would watch my back with them, but at the same time I felt they had my back when needed.

We met the Ontario-based hard rock band Sven Gali when they were playing in New York City. They were about the same age and had the same hunger as us. Their debut album would go Gold in Canada, which means it sold between 40-80,000 copies. We liked each other's music and I got to know their manager who got us a three week Canadian tour centered around Winnipeg and Thunder Bay. It was a fun outing that got noticed by the <u>Winnipeg Sun</u>. They described us as "hard-rockin', black-wearin' vampires" with an original sound that fused the sound of Mötley Crüe, New York heavy metal band Riot and 70's band Nazareth with the "energy of speed-metal" to create an "incendiary device ready to explode." My "acrobatics" and "menacing histrionics" were compared to Ian Astbury, Jim Morrison and Sebastian Bach. I'll take all of that, and thank you.

Though, it wasn't all fun. We vampires were almost stopped in our tracks before we crawled out of our coffins and got started on the hard rock feast. We had a crazy drive to the border split between a car and a 16 passenger van we'd rented. I was in the van with our drummer and gear. We hit an obscure border crossing in Minnesota that shut down at night, meaning we were forced to uncomfortably sleep in the vehicles until morning.

The next morning as my drummer and I were about to cross, the border patrol agents got a little curious about some of us. They pulled both vehicles over and found marijuana seeds and smoking paraphernalia in the van. I didn't know it was there, but wasn't surprised knowing my bandmate. As the narcotics dogs appeared time suddenly seemed to stop. Things weren't made easier by the discovery that the band t-shirts we had to sell at the gigs get charged duty, so we were out of money before starting. This is why bands have merch produced in the destination country, and won't bring the unsold items back with them. Anything not sold is taxed, killing the profits.

Our drummer regularly had a bad attitude and thought he was funny when he often wasn't. He thought he was a rock star already. He even destroyed hotel rooms, which we paid for on an income that wasn't budgeted for that level of rock star foolishness. He looked at the border agents and cockily asked,

"Whose going to give me an anal cavity search?" This was heard by an old man who casually came out of the building to us and said, "I will." He took the drummer away, while the rest of us suffered more than enough as the vehicles got searched. By the time we returned to the States a few weeks later I was pretty upset at my drummer for putting us into a potentially bad situation that could have been far worse.

Some months later we had a couple shows booked in Toronto. I had a friend with a delivery service in Manhattan who loaned me his Ford Bronco and a pick-up truck with a cab for our stuff, while joining us to sell our band t-shirts which he'd made. On the way back home in his pick-up was the two of us and a Canadian friend of his I didn't know well. At the border the agents asked each of us where we were coming from and going and what our business was. They asked the Canadian fellow what he was doing. "I'm going to New York City for vacation." The agent how much money he had. "20 dollars." The agent asked if he had any credit cards. "Nope." The agent then asked us to pull over, as who goes on vacation to one of America's most expensive cities with not even enough money for a hotel. Nobody with legitimate intentions it became glaringly obvious to me as I had flashbacks.

My drummer was driving my friend's truck and I called him over the walkie-talkies we had. I asked him to wait for us, as I didn't know what was going to happen. He said he'd drive a mile, pull over and wait to hear from me. As soon as he was out of sight the agent said the Canadian fellow couldn't cross and we needed to bring him back to Toronto. I figured my friend could take him back and I'd just have my drummer come back and get me. I had a job I needed to get back to, while my friend was his own boss and could handle better being late back to work.

Luck was not with me, yet again. My drummer didn't stop, or if he did he didn't wait long for my call, but kept driving back home. I don't know which, as when I called him there was response. I thus had to go back to Toronto, which cost us so much time I was forced to stay there overnight. On the way back the pair of us got through the border fine, but we were caught in a crazy rain storm that forced us into a hotel for a night. Three days later I finally got home exhausted, low on cash and as frustrated as anything, plus seriously late for work. I got home to my roommate, who was also the drummer, and before I could say anything he says, "Don't even talk to me about anything." In less than a minute I was done with him in what was a huge wake-up call over his selfishness. He'd left me behind in a foreign country, pretty much stole my friend's Bronco albeit temporarily, gotten us stopped for drugs and was just a jerk. He was immediately fired.

In the years since I've gone to Canada for shows with other bands. Going across an international border is a stressful situation on a basic level, particularly in a world post-9/11, and can quickly and easily transform into a time drain and headache. Since Naked City I've always had a contract my bandmates have to sign to protect myself and the band as a corporate entity. The contract holds them personally liable for anything, illegal or otherwise, that leads to canceled gigs and unexpected additional expenses. It might seem extreme, but I've never had any problems since.

The life of a rock band is one that follows a series of well-trodden steps up. We were set to hit the next one up when we landed a gig at CBGB's. While it might not have had the excitement of the first two times I played there with Avant Garde, and since then I'd spent a lot of time hanging out at the club, I was still very excited to play there again. For Avant Garde it was a bit of an experiment to see what might happen, but for Naked City we were hot and people were taking notice of us. We had been told a couple label executives would be in the audience explicitly to see us. The big break had finally fallen into my lap after countless ups and down. I could see it on the horizon as clear as the sun rise.

4

DAZED & CONFUSED

This path has led me to some of the darkest places I've ever been, but I think that was already in me, anyway. I think being a musician you get the opportunity to work it out.
~ Ian Astbury

We just blew it.

There is no other way to describe the most important gig in the life of Naked City. This was our big moment and we blew it, knew it and then made it worse. Ironically, the guys who had the biggest bragging mouths in the band were the ones that blew it for all of us. They tore the naked city to the ground to the point of having nothing to brag about.

The drummer choked. On some level I can't blame him too harshly. We were all really nervous. But, his nerves caused him to mess up the timing of our song 'My Little Sapphire.' This knocked all of us off course. By the time the song came to a sad disjointed end both the song and the energy of the performance was ruined.

Then, during another song one of my guitar players whipped off his shirt and fell down on his knees while playing. Maybe he thought he was Jimi Hendrix or someone famous in that moment, or maybe he was trying to make up for the earlier energy crash that never really left us. It was not the right moment for that. There may not have been any right moment for that.

I'm looking over at him on the ground and I knew right then what he did. He blew the gig. Looking at the audience told me they were no longer with us. After all the countless hours of performing with the band I could read an audience. There was no more energy in the air to magically shift around.

Was I ever pissed. I'd been working hard and putting in my best, but my success was just as much under my control as it was in the hands of my bandmates. They'd pissed away my chance at something, as much as their own. Don and Jonathan did not speak to us for several weeks. That made it worse knowing we'd failed not just ourselves and the audience, but also our managers.

Truthfully, we were right at the end of the hair band era. As soon as the grunge came it was hard to get a deal for hard rock bands, then hip-hop got huge and pushed our style of music out even more. Yet, we almost had a deal. The people who could have made it happen were right there waiting to be awed that night. Maybe it might not have turned into something huge or lasted long, but it would have been something. It would have been the proper climax for all that I'd worked for and wanted since I was singing the Beatles on the radio. Then it wasn't there and it likely wasn't going to be there again given the changing music scene.

It so wasn't there that Naked City broke up soon after. Unlike Avant Garde where we hit a crossroads, this was just the end of the road. The gig was too important and the tragedy and embarrassment too much. As could be expected, the drummer bailed on us and moved on to another project. We played our few last shows with a different drummer, Joey Crifo, who wound up playing with the popular New York City band Speed McQueen.

After that, Don, being the good manager he was who was always looking at the future and not dwelling on the past, pushed me to do a solo project. He knew I wasn't the cause of the band's failure and there was still potential to be tapped in my singing. It was just time to try something new and maybe not rely on others. He wanted to keep managing me, and hoped for a showcase gig that would lead to being signed with a label as a solo singer. I was kinda bummed over Naked City, but I followed his lead and instincts. He worked it out so I could audition and rehearse my new solo band at Don Hill's during the day before it opened.

I found myself forming a new band with musicians I didn't know. He was recommending people to me to audition. It didn't gel. I wasn't feeling it. There was no camaraderie like I had gotten used to with Naked City, while none of us were quite on the same page to make up for the lack of a personal history together.

I was living hand to mouth. My new group of players were all in the same boat as me. We were all struggling to get noticed and none of us had reached the big league yet. We all loved making music, but we weren't making much money with it. Yet, some of the musicians Don was sending to me had turned big league before their time. They were asking for perks that a big name musician might ask for, except they weren't big names. They assumed that since they had talent that granted them other wishes. I would have liked to have been a part of that reality, too, but I had my feet too planted on the ground to pretend that was the way the world worked.

I had an eighteen year old prima donna guitarist who wanted me to pay for his parking as he was coming in from Long Island. I was like, "You should be happy with what you've got." He got noticed by a top notch manager. This didn't mean he was suddenly a star. Don't make demands day one, particularly when its no secret there is no money. There were other frustrating requests, like if I could change rehearsals to the evening at a time more convenient for one person. No, we were guests in someone's club that had bands booked at night. We were lucky we had a free place to rehearse in a city where bands pay by the hour to have a small poorly ventilated rehearsal space. Or, I had a drummer who came to audition and the first thing he wanted was to go get a beer. Are you here to drink or play?

It seemed the members of my solo band were either prematurely professional or not professional enough. Don didn't want to hear their complaints and I didn't want to either. It just put a bad taste in my mouth and soured the project before it got started.

My only attempt at a solo career came to an unceremonious end due to the bassist. There was no failed gig at CBGB's this time, as we never got beyond the rehearsal stage. All she did was smoke pot and get too high to focus on playing properly. On St. Patrick's Day the two of us with Don went over to another club he was a co-owner of and where many of his music industry friends hung out. This was his turf and a place of influential people. My bassist started making out with with the co-owner's girlfriend and making a huge scene. Not just was it embarrassing, but it got Don got angry. I'd had enough problems and with Don now angry and embarrassed my limit was hit and the solo project officially over.

One thing I refuse to do is be anyone's babysitter. That's what I felt I was doing through this whole solo project and it came to a head that night. I don't want to, let alone won't, look after anyone cause they are too high to function and be responsible. I just wanted to write and put something cool together, but it was too hard. Its nearly impossible to be fully creative and a babysitter at the same time. The only thing that came out of a solo career was a hard lesson in what I wanted and didn't want in a band moving forward.

Of course, I know this may all feel hypocritical on some level, because I liked to party and chase girls like anyone, and had my share of drunken irresponsible moments. Yet, through it all I had day jobs to pay the bills. I was also always was on stage or in rehearsals as required and expected. Music was my priority, not living a crazy lifestyle.

I had another music experience during this time that went nowhere, though I'm not sure whose fault it really is. Luck was not on my side in these months after Naked City.

I saw an ad for someone to sing on a hard rock album along the musical lines of Ronnie James Dio. I contacted the guy. He sent me some music, which I liked, and I responded with my ideas for lyrics and vocal melodies. Him and his bandmate agreed to fly me to Florida, near Jacksonville, for an audition to feel me out further. I was told to be prepared to start recording immediately once I got to the studio straight from the airport. Coming off a long airplane ride and slogging through airports might not be the best time to create vocal magic, but I'd give it my best if they were that gung-ho. Plus, they were paying me a few thousand, so I was pretty much saying yes to everything.

They had this house they shared where they'd build a studio. I started singing and recording and offering the ideas that I had. We spent about five hours doing music before it was time to call it a night. These guys smoked so much pot it was insane, but it seemed like a good audition. I had a hotel and would return home the next day.

The next morning I came back to the studio and there was this weird energy. I was told, "We're not really too happy with what happened." What happened? "You didn't do what you were supposed to do. You were out of key and didn't sing well."

What? They had a list of complaints. I said its an audition. It's not going to be perfect, nor expected to be. Auditions aren't perfect by their nature.

That's where I was wrong. What I saw as an audition, they saw as me being officially hired to record a final product. I don't know where the communication breakdown happened or if they were never clear to start with. Maybe through their pot haze they thought things had been clear. For them I had clearly failed in upholding my side of the bargain. I was flabbergasted. They were straight up angry. Though they generously said I could keep the money

With the amount of pot they smoked I started to get seriously scared. I just wanted to leave. They were going to take me to the airport, but had to get their van fixed first. I waited around with them for five hours until they could take me. It was a nerve-wracking uncomfortable five hours. There went my newest band, a band I didn't actually know I was a part of.

I learned a lot from my years with Avant Garde, Naked City and my other music endeavors. I learned what failure felt like. I learned how much people are busting their butts to become rock stars and how hard it actually is. Those who are successful work hard for it and suffer for it. It doesn't fall into one's lap and nobody can party their way into success, or any success that will add up to much or last long. Plus, there's a lot of false starts and unexpected variables that pull one back to square one with few or no consolation prizes. Just being in a big city like New York is only part of the equation to becoming a rock star, or having a career of any sort in music. It doesn't guarantee success. Being in a band requires wearing the hats of artist, musician, businessman, therapist and likely more. Its not all glamour and fun like my fashion illustration portrayed it as I learned.

This is not to mention that big dreams are great, but most of us have bills to pay. Living in the city none of us ever really had a lot of money and savings never lasted long. Even when money was coming in from our gigs the end result was often a break even or loss or there were unexpected expenditures, like the 3 days it took to get back from Toronto. Though, to my own fault and nearsightedness, partying regularly also drains the coffers, while I wasn't giving my art career as much dedication as my nightlife and music career. I always did art to keep my head above water financially, but I could have taken it more seriously. There were good opportunities I turned down that would have interfered with the music. In hindsight, those opportunities likely would have increased my stability and reduced some financial stress, which might have actually put me in a healthier mental place leading to better energy put into my music. The benefits would have undoubtedly outweighed any loss that having a larger daytime commitment would have caused. I didn't see that relationship then.

When I first moved to New York City I worked for an ad agency across from Andy Warhol's Factory, and had other art jobs for different companies of various types. Don would sometimes hook me up with art projects for some extra cash. I did lots of stuff for a psychic and metaphysician uptown named Biond Fury. I designed for him a set a tarot cards, a Ouija board, drew different things for him that he'd would use in his work. He claimed to have a close tie with John Lennon, and owned a raccoon jacket said to be his. He'd later become a well-known dealer of Beatles memorabilia, including owning the white suit Lennon wore crossing Abbey Road. On top of the spiritual stuff he was trying to make a record and do a whole multi-media thing fusing spirituality and entertainment. I was helping him with it, along with my guitarist friend Jimi K. Bones. It may not have been the most lucrative day job, but all I saw was how it was one of the few jobs that was developing my music.

I met Jimi during Naked City days and he became a close friend. I had a girlfriend who shared an apartment with him and his girlfriend. His band Skin N' Bones traveled the same circles as Naked City and we were like buddy bands, but they had a record deal. Between the bands and the girlfriends Jimi and I were interacting all the time. His girlfriend worked for a record company that worked with the Scorpions, while Jimi was also a substitute guitarist in glam band Kix who had been signed since 1981. Music was all the time and everything with all of us.

Working for the psychic was a job I really enjoyed and it didn't interfere with the band, but I had other jobs that were less than glamorous. There was a car show at the Javits Convention Center that overlooks the Hudson River. I needed money and was hired to walk around with a sign hanging off me for a nearby car shop doing refurbishments. I did it for an hour, then some guy rudely told me how much they were paying me to look like an asshole. That was it. I was done. I felt I didn't need the money that bad. I probably did, but my pride was huge and my decision making questionable these days.

    The months following the collapse of Naked City were not good days for me. The anxiety was intense. I couldn't see any way forward. I couldn't see any way out. I could barely figure out how to survive, let alone escape my dour predicament and get to better situations and opportunities, if they even existed. My music career was stagnant for the first time since leaving college.

    For those that live or have lived in New York City they understand that the city has its own level of ever-present anxiety that seeps under the skin and adds to whatever stress one already is facing. Living in one of the country's most expensive cities while struggling in near poverty isn't a winning combination. Not having a steady job just makes things worse. Its ironic that the city is a hub of the music industry, yet so many musicians are living hand to mouth. They might be able to survive easier elsewhere in cheaper environments, but then they'd be out of reach of the movers and shakers. Its a painful relationship of constant struggle. If I thought about moving out of the city to calmer pastures I couldn't figure out how to make it happen. How does one get out of a hole when its impossible to see anything to hold on to to lift one's self up with? Moving down to Florida with my parents was not an option for many reasons.

    I had lost my band of many years, missed my big break a couple times, had a solo career fail, and screwed up an audition with a band that obviously had money to burn. To top it off my girlfriend said she didn't want to break-up, but could I move somewhere else? Less a maybe and more an insistence. I moved into this woman's loft, thinking we were still dating but just not living together anymore. I was naively duped.

    What was the next thing that was going to fall apart and take the floor out from under me? I didn't want to think about. Its no understatement to say I was quite literally wandering around dazed and confused.

5

THE OCEAN

You've got this thing inside you where you know there's something around the corner that you've never heard before, but who's going to pick the lock to get it out?
~ Robert Plant

Its interesting how life drops things into one's lap when everything appears to be at its lowest. About six months had gone by since Naked City collapsed when Don said he had opportunity for me to get signed to a major label. The best part? How would I like to go to Japan? Before I knew it my music career was on the rise again like a phoenix, and ironically in the land of the Rising Sun. I went from nothing to being in a meeting with Don and some Japanese businessmen, and less than a month later on an airplane to Tokyo.

Hiro Kuretani, a Japanese drummer who was also into early computer/electronica music, was in the audience for a Naked City show at the Cat Club, Don told me. He and his producer, a woman named Yasumi Takeuchi, had an idea for a proggy hard rock band that would include two Americans and two Japanese musicians. He already had a guitarist in Makoto "Mac" Mizunuma, who had an Eddie Van Halen-esque style, and he wanted me to front the band and write the lyrics. He had a label back home in Japan already supporting the new project.

Yasumi went everywhere Hiro went. She was our manager, our producer, and our boss. She was also the literal voice of Hiro and Mac. Hiro spoke limited English and Mac none. She was the machine driving the whole project.

The band was to be called World XXI. The World is the twenty-first tarot card and means completion of a journey, but also new beginnings. Of course, the name tapped into my spiritual interests and felt somewhat fated. Though, interestingly, to some Japanese the XXI would be considered English and not Roman. Translation fumbles ensued as they tried to pronounce our name. Nothing is perfect, but I'd encountered far worse problems and this one made me chuckle.

So, while I thought Naked City had missed our chance and driven away label interest, actually it had ended up being my chance. Things had been brewing for my career without my knowledge all this time. The future suddenly looked very bright. The seeds sowed come back in the weirdest and most unexpected ways sometimes.

My first stop was Los Angeles to meet Mac and Hiro and audition bassists. We decided on Dave Crigger. He'd spent four years touring with a reunited Foghat, known for the hit 'Slow Ride', and had been in a band with Megadeth guitarist Jeff Young. I believe Dave was always on the short list, and like myself was being investigated long before they made contact. In one listen it doesn't take long to realize why they were interested in him. He had this quasi-lead bass style that mixed traditional fingerstyle with a slap and pop technique commonly found with jazz players and, at that time, a small circle of rock bassists like Flea and Les Claypool of Primus. His style both provided the traditional bass line and drove the music like John Entwistle of the Who and Billy Sheehan, who was called the Eddie Van Halen of the bass. We were lucky to have Dave's talent and unique style.

Hiro and Yasumi and their label were wanting to break into the American market with World XXI. Their label did all these compilation albums of previously released tracks by American rappers, like Dr. Dre, Ice T, 2 Live Crew. These were essentially cash grabs, as they only had to pay license fees, with the musicians likely not even knowing of their existence. World XXI was their investment in something bigger with actual musicians they could directly work with and grow. There was no limits to the potential.

Its a different ballgame now with the internet, but in the '90's American labels weren't interested in Japanese bands. Japanese bands had trouble getting in the door. Grunge would make it even more difficult to get a foot in the door. Let alone, once they were in they faced the difficulty of staying relevant and in the eye of American audiences. Living across the ocean meant they were out of the scene except when touring, let alone behind a language barrier. Having two American guys who called America home was a strong selling point, plus we had connections here they didn't. While it might seem shocking, I didn't feel like I was used at all in this situation. The experience brought me to Japan and it gave me a great opportunity to create new and different music with some serious players. It was more like an exchange where we all brought something to the table and we all benefited.

Dave and I spent about six months in Japan writing and rehearsing with Hiro and Mac. We were put up in the same hotel, but in rooms on opposite sides of the building. I was paid about a $2000 a month salary, which was plenty given many of our living expenses were covered.

My daily routine was I'd exercise after getting up, take a walk, go to rehearsals which always included a catered lunch, then rehearse for about six hours. Dave met a woman, Rika Himenogi, who was a famous Japanese teen pop singer. He'd go off with her and I would often explore Japan on my own, or watch Japanese TV, or be writing lyrics in my room. Though, its funny, Dave was a boxing buff. He actually had a VCR and tapes of boxing matches shipped to Japan from America.

I absolutely loved Japan. I thought the Japanese people were an amazing people. I loved the experience of getting to create music in that environment with something new and interesting coming to me nearly everyday. It was very inspiring. It didn't hurt that all the expenses were paid, a rare job perk, allowing me finally have that moment of financial stability.

Hiro and Mac had the music largely sketched out before Dave and I joined. It was my job to write the lyrics and create the vocal melodies. Hiro gave me some ideas for lyrics, like he told me the story that created 'El Dorado'. Dave's bass style was a great bridge between my melodies and Mac's guitar parts.

We went to Los Angeles to record the album. We had about fifteen songs in total with eleven making it to the CD. We spent two weeks at American Recording Studios. We worked with engineer Bill Cooper. At that time he was famous for production work with such classic acts as Alice Cooper, Iron Butterfly, Three Dog Night and Steppenwolf, though he would go on to work with blues icon John Mayall, Motorhead and step into the world of classical music.

Hiro is more artistic when it comes to playing than what can be heard on our album. He reminded me of a Japanese Neil Peart. His interest in electronics and the early experimental computer music sadly didn't really get tapped into with World XXI. He wanted the music to be different than what it turned into. I wouldn't call what he wanted rock jazz fusion, just a more intricate and ethereal type of music like he was personally interested in, but Yasumi was pushing the hard rock thing. I think he was getting frustrated with the hard rock we ended up doing, that it didn't push the limit more. Or, at least, he seemed frustrated at times. At the same time Dave, Mac and him put some pretty amazing stuff together that we were all proud of.

He'd get heavier and get to experiment in his next band Vertex, with frontman Stephen Pearcy of Ratt and guitarist Al Pitrelli of Megadeth and Trans-Siberian Orchestra. Though, he did manage to slip in a little experimenting in with us. Hiro's drumming might sound ordinary on the CD, but his tools were not. He had Mercedes Benz wheel spokes clicking like a hi-hat. The sound of the hi-hat heard on our album will never be heard anywhere else.

We went back to Japan and did some rehearsals, leading to a couple trial shows in Tokyo. This was followed by a handful of shows around the country, yet the crowds were more than a handful with 1000 person shows in Tokyo to several thousand in Nagoya and Osaka. We opened for the legendary drummer Carmine Appice. He co-wrote 'Do You Think I'm Sexy' with Rod Stewart and played with Jeff Beck, along with a whose who of '70's rock stars. He was touring his band that featured bassist Tony Franklin, guitarist Mitch Perry, and Kelly Keeling singing and playing keyboards. Keeling, who would go on to sing with Trans-Siberian Orchestra, wasn't too nice. Perry, who has played with the Michael Schenker Group and Edgar Winter, came off with a huge ego who was also not the nicest guy. We almost got into a fight at our show in Nagoya. My love of playing practical jokes didn't help band relations. I'd found a joke store in Japan and gotten some gum that snaps back into the package. Being the big shot he just totally grabbed it and it snapped back. I think he was going to punch me if it wasn't for Carmine stepping in with his big Italian presence. Carmine, on the other hand, I got along with really well. While Tony was a very quiet guy. Everyone knows him from playing in the Firm, the band that featured Paul Rodgers of Bad Company and Jimmy Page. If only I knew I'd eventually be playing in a Zeppelin tribute band I might have asked him some questions about Jimmy.

Aside from backstage shenanigans, they were great shows. The tour acted as album promotions for both of bands, labeled as the 'Super Rock Session'. Motorhead was touring Japan and hitting the same venues just before us. It was wild seeing a huge American band in Japan and then getting to perform on the same stage within days.

It was also great playing with the guys. Dave was phenomenal. Hiro and Mac were amazing. We were also incredibly tight due to our daily rehearsals. These were also the days when I still did a lot of running and climbing around and jumping into the crowd, so they were high energy shows all around.

How far I'd come. Here I was touring Japan promoting the first album to have my lyrics and voice, I had a band of professional top notch musicians behind me, I didn't need a non-musical day job to survive, I was hanging out backstage and touring with rock royalty, and the next step on the itinerary was a short tour of America to promote our album. I was becoming a rock star. I was living my dream. It only took a few false starts, but I actually made it this time.

6

GALLOWS POLE

In the early part of my time in Zeppelin I wrote naively, but I loved all that mystery of the dark past and the Queen of Light. Unfortunately, I had it taken away from me bit by bit.
~ Robert Plant

Before starting the American tour I went back to Los Angeles on my own for two weeks to rewrite and re-record my vocals for the American version of the album, which would also get a new mix. The American version would be self-titled, while the Japanese version had the name XXI. The American release never got much traction. Neither version of the CD did, actually. Honestly, like Avant Garde, our timing was off. The Stone Temple Pilots were coming in and there was no place for our style of proggy melodic hard rock. One reviewer described us as bluesy hard rock like Lynch Mob. None of those descriptors were in our favor. Perhaps if Hiro had been able to experiment more, things might have been different, but Yasumi clung to an image of a dying music scene that she pushed on us. Maybe she didn't know it was fading from her distant view in Japan.

Yet, even though we were out of sync with the trends, the experience of re-recording the vocals skyrocketed me as a singer. The Japanese label was going to have Music Mine, Co. in Los Angeles release the album in America, except the staff of Music Mine wanted to re-do my vocals and re-mix the album. Some additional guitar and keyboard parts were also added.

I worked with the great songwriter and producer Warren Croyle, aka Mr. Reality. He's not so well-known, but has a production resume that includes obscure groups like the thrash band Uncle Sham and Japanese fusion group Hiroshima, while later working with popular groups Gwar and Mercy Playground. Today he works as a producer and director on indie films and documentaries.

Warren was a wacky alpha male. His direction had a very intimidating edge, yet he was so creative and it was so educational for me that I followed his lead with unflinching trust in his vision. We worked out of the garage that had been converted into a studio by the drummer of White Lion, who had broken up a few years previous. He was cool, but always seemed to be in the kitchen when we were there.

Warren really helped me to improve the lyrics and rework the vocal melodies. He also helped me become a better singer in general. He really knew what he was doing when it came to melodies, whereas the Japanese didn't understand my lyrics and thus they focused mostly on my pitch. The worst criticism of my singing I had ever received came while we were recording the demos in Japan. It wasn't meant as bad, and was more a language barrier issue. The Japanese said I had too much vibrato. I was trying hard to control it. Its different than it is today where I'm more aware of how to use and control my voice, which finds its roots in Warren's tutelage. Yet, at that time the Japanese production team very well might have been right, but in the end I was frustrated and they were frustrated. They couldn't get me to do what they wanted and I couldn't understand what they wanted. Eventually they said I should try to sound like Eddie Vedder. Are you kidding me? He's nothing but vibrato. He's like singing while on a bus. I'd been largely left to my own devices in Japan, and not allowed to make changes when we did the final album, but with Warren I was wailing and feeling great.

Warren was mentoring me as much as working with and directing me. He helped my vocal presentation in ways that I would tap into for years to come. He showed me a really helpful decongestant mix that prevents the throat from locking up, supposedly used by the Black Crowes. Also, between him and the Japanese attention to getting the perfect tones, I found before rehearsals I would have to do scales and vocal exercises. I'd never done that before. I believe the whole recording experience with World XXI got me really good with my vocal quality, putting me on another level, not to mention building my confidence. It taught me what I was good at and where I was weak. I'm really glad to have had his mentorship.

I think World XXI wrote some great songs, but on the Japanese version the mix is bad and my vocals are terrible. On its own its doesn't sound so bad, but when compared to the American version it becomes painfully obvious. The Japanese version is a gritty progressive metal album with lots of extended musical parts, that I feel was targeted to guitarists who like highly technical music. Warren masterfully turned it into something more accessible and '80's. It hits hard and fierce with an edginess that at times sounds like Judas Priest, but also has a groove the Japanese version completely lacks. Warren took the music to new places.

Just after our Japanese tour ended Dave quit the band and went back to America. He eventually married Rika and became a family man, with one of his kids taking up the drums. It was a major loss for us musically.

Plans for the American leg hit another snag as Mac couldn't join us. I never was told why and I'd never talked to him again to discover why.

Hiro and Yasumi joined me in New York City, as I pulled out my address book to find some replacement members. Young bands often lose members, so I wasn't too worried, though Dave had a style that wasn't easily replaceable. I brought in my old bassist Kurt from Naked City and guitarist Bruce Edwards from the Don Hill's house band, not to be confused with jazz guitarist Bruce Edwards of Sun Ra's Arkestra. Kurt had a very different style, but did really good, while Bruce was a top caliber guitarist. So while there was a sound change, I was feeling good about moving forward with the new line-up. It was great having my old friends join me on this new endeavor, and to be able to share my success with them. We rehearsed and then hit the road for two and a half months for about twenty shows around the country.

What really happened was we didn't so much hit the road, but hit wall after wall after wall. It was an unmitigated disaster.

Maybe I shouldn't have been as shocked and frustrated as I became as the days on the road dragged painfully on. The signs were actually there for awhile that things were not all that they seemed, but I hadn't put any weight into them if I even saw them for what they were. Dave saw the signs and added them up. He also had issues that I didn't have, such as the album liner notes didn't list the instrument endorsements he had. Part of the endorsement deal requires they be listed, but they don't appear on either version. The guitar and drum endorsements of Hiro and Mac do appear on the Japanese version, interestingly enough.

When we were recording the album in Los Angeles there was a note on the studio wall that specifically indicated that all production decisions were to be made by Hiro and Hiro alone. Nobody could have any creative input aside from him. We had to duplicate our parts from the demos exactly as they were with no changes. It was a little frustrating, as its common to want to make changes after having a chance to reflect on the demos. This was part of the reason why working with Warren was so enjoyable, as he allowed the normal back-and-forth creativity.

Then, while we were doing the shows in Japan we had some publishing disagreements. I asked to have listed in the album's liner notes that all the lyrics were written by me. Hiro and Yasumi told me at a show in Tokyo that this wasn't going to happen. By not giving me credit they could claim all the publishing royalties for the lyrics. Hiro was already splitting composing royalties with Dave and Mac. Hiro gave me ideas for some of the songs, though credit for the concepts to all the songs is given to him on the Japanese version, but all the lyrics were completely mine or shared with Warren. Warren only got credit for remixing and producing, and no songwriting credit. I said I was going to get on a plane the next day and leave the band if I didn't get the publishing rights that were rightly due me. I got really angry, so they made sure to give me credit for all the lyrics. When we were touring I also received a small portion of the publishing from the label.

In hindsight, I wonder if they gave me the credit just to calm me down so they could do the shows unhindered. Finding a replacement American rock singer in Japan who could learn the songs in a matter of hours would be a real life miracle, so I was largely irreplaceable.

Yasumi was a machine that wanted as much power and control as she could get to achieve some grand scheme I can only guess at. I do not believe the success of World XXI was her ultimate priority. Hiro went with it like a puppet, allowing himself to be pushed around. I'm sure she was behind him having complete creative control in the studio. She was doing a lot of sneaky things, which I saw after the fact. She even got our first management fired.

Dave has since called her a Japanese devil. I call her our very own Yoko Ono, but in our case our John had no professional experience and unflinchingly did everything Yoko wanted. My interpreter from Polydor Records later said Yasumi was directly to blame for the publishing hassle. The record company had no issues with me getting all the royalties. She had no real experience as a producer. Her work had included producing some of the compilation rap albums, but that didn't involve creating the music, just putting together the packaging without any artist input and giving herself a fancy production credit. Her lack of inexperience mixed with a bloated sense of importance and desire for power was the band's Achilles heal.

Now here we were in America and the problems snowballed like an avalanche. Yasumi hired an American publicity company that was a scam. They were either completely incompetent, or knew what they were doing and took advantage of the fact their clients were naive Japanese in unfamiliar surroundings. It might also be likely that Yasumi had dug her claws into them and they were serving up a plate of just deserts. To this day I do not actually know what happened behind the scenes. The only thing I do know is that they royally screwed the band over.

I knew we'd been scammed the moment all of us were waiting with our gear and luggage on a busy sidewalk in Midtown Manhattan and the guy from the company pulls up in a rented Ryder moving truck. We were to put our stuff in the back, except the driver didn't have a lock. An unlocked vehicle with music equipment is a theft just waiting to happen. Musicians often get their gear stolen, even when probably locked up.

It got worse. He expected us to ride in the back with our stuff. No way! Over two months in the summer in the back of a poorly ventilated, dark and unsafe Ryder moving truck is pure insanity. I fired the guy right on the spot and became our tour manager. I should have realized right there that if the company couldn't get proper transportation then the days to follow were going to be a slow ride through hell with me at the wheel and no road map.

What a ride through hell it was. We would show up at venues, but the club would have no clue who we were. There was no booking for us, if there was even a show scheduled for the night. Not quite half of the bookings were like this. We had an agenda in our hands that was just words on a page with names out of a phone book. Often the club would slot us in for the night, most likely out of pity. Except it would be as the first act of the night, meaning it was too early for any crowd to turn up. While no booking also meant there had been no publicity about us playing, thus nobody was there to see us. The fact that some of the clubs were not much to write home about was just frosting on the cake.

The train wreck masquerading as a tour was a constant hustle by me to salvage the moment. I wasn't going to drive from state to state and not perform nor make money, so I did whatever I could to get us on stage at every venue we were supposedly scheduled at. To make matters worse, at one point Yasumi got Hiro a personal assistant. I was busting my ass on and off stage and quite seriously suffering for my art. Did I get any help from Yasumi? Nope. Did I get any extra money for taking on extra roles? Nope. What was Hiro doing that required him to need a personal assistant? Nothing that I could think of. Talk about getting screwed over in a passive/aggressive way.

During our few months touring the Coast and mid-Atlantic states we opened for Quiet Riot for a handful of shows. I got to meet the guys. That was cool, as during my college years I was almost in a Quiet Riot cover band. We also opened a few shows for Arcade, heavy alt-rock band formed by singer Stephen Pearcy after Ratt disbanded. He was on a low and transitional part of his career between Ratt and starting a solo career. He was like in his own little haze the few chances I had to talk with him.

World XXI can take the prize for having the worst gig of my life, even to the present day. We were schedule in Des Moines, Iowa with Quiet Riot and a local band. Our previous gig was over a week earlier in Charlotte, North Carolina. We took our time to drive up through the states and enjoy the views. We arrived at the venue and I immediately set out to figure out what the situation was. I had no information when we were supposed to go on. We got screwed over, as we were scheduled to open and then the local band and then Quiet Riot. The rule of thumb in this situation is that the local band is the usual opener of the evening. The first band usually has the smallest crowd, as folks often arrive late to just see the headliner.

While I was arguing with the agents, having been told we'd go on in our proper place as the second band, Kurt tells me we have another problem. He didn't have his bass effects. He thought he'd left them in Charlotte. He hadn't once gone to pull out his gear while on the road. He had to run out and hunt down a music store and buy about $500 worth of new gear. There went his income for the night.

By the time we ended our set I was frustrated beyond belief. I drank a lot and got mad. I was too frustrated to see Quiet Riot's performance, who I had wanted to see. I was just screaming and freaking out in the car as we pulled away. I was working really hard for crappy situations and people who were off their rocker. While my guitarist wanted to look for strip clubs in every town. He also was from England and wanted vanilla malts at every restaurant. Good luck finding those in small town America. I was scrambling for the band as well as my sanity, while Hiro had an assistant and Yasumi acted all innocent smiles and my guitarist wanted milkshakes and strippers. This was not the rock star life I had envisioned for myself.

The tour finally ended. Hiro and Yasumi were going back to Japan, but I'd stay in the States and get things ready for another tour of America and Japan. We even had a party at Hiro's hotel in Times Square to kick off the future tour. Even after the disaster Kurt was in. Bruce couldn't do it, so I hired from my Naked City days guitarist Michael Angelo. I'd get in touch with Hiro by October to start touring that month. Kurt, Michael and I put it on our calendars and rehearsals were planned, while I camped out in Jimi Bones' apartment.

"We'll talk to you guys in October," was the last thing Hiro ever said to me. Come October my phone calls were never returned and no calls from Japan were forthcoming. I found out through the grapevine that World XXI was dead. I got a call from one of the Los Angeles Music Mine, Co. guys threatening me with a lawsuit for something I knew nothing about, and had nothing to do with once I figured out the situation. His situation could be traced back to Yasumi's continual sabotage, while I fast discovered I was without a band. The official verification came not with a call from Japan, as one might expect, but when my money stopped coming in soon after the tour ended. They left me hanging forgotten from the gallows pole.

I was pissed. I was embarrassed. I had Michael and Kurt counting on me who were also out of a gig and income source. Everyone had blocked off their calendars and they had potentially passed on other opportunities. I was frustrated and they were frustrated. It wasn't my fault, but the people to blame were far out of reach never to be seen or heard from again.

World XXI was completely over. Hiro didn't dismiss me and reform with new musicians. He just killed the band completely with not even a thank you and goodbye note. Even with Yasumi's power tripping I was not expecting to be treated like that. Perhaps I was naive, but I was not expecting to be tossed away so casually, particularly after all I'd done to keep the band alive on the road.

In the years since I've never seen a penny of the rest of the publishing owed me, though the album is still available in Japan. The publishing stopped with the other income. Hiro and Yasumi fraudulently took all the money, just like they always planned. They may still be receiving publishing that should be coming to me. Its a thorn in my side and something I've looked into rectifying, but I just don't know the avenue to take to get my publishing from a foreign corporation.

About a year later I discovered Hiro was in a new experimental industrial metal trio with Stephen Pearcy and Al Pitrelli called Vertex, with Robbie Crane joining them on stage. They did an album that was poorly received by fans expecting something less alienating, followed by a short tour with Manowar. They folded with no fanfare when Stephen joined a Ratt reunion, bringing with him Robbie for a new era of the iconic band. It was almost a repeat of World XXI with creative sessions with top notch players, a tour with a famous band, only to have it crash fairly quickly with no real commercial success or album distribution.

Vertex played in Manhattan and I almost went to the gig. After much inner debate I decided against it. I was still too angry and burned. It was better for my sanity that I stay away.

It didn't make the past any better when I discovered that while I'd been pushing World XXI through a tour of hell Yasumi was going behind my back luring in Stephen to work with Hiro, likely with lots of fake smiles and empty promises of future success. The fact that Stephen's band Arcade was struggling and eventually dropped by Epic was everything Yasumi likely could have wanted to secure the last nail in the coffin of World XXI. I have nothing against Stephen, who went with an interesting new opportunity when his career was at a low point. God bless him for doing exactly what I did and would have done in his shoes. He likely didn't know who I was or what was going on.

    I don't know if Yasumi and Hiro ever really planned for World XXI to last, or maybe it was just a way to get to America and find bigger and better opportunities and more famous people to work with. If Stephen hadn't been around I don't know if we would have stayed together. Yasumi might have found some other American rock star to sink her talons into, thus the dissolution of the band was likely destined to happen at some point. Though, at the time, I thought we easily could have gone a few years. Without her we might have.

7

TRAMPLED UNDER FOOT

The idea of spending a year and a half in the studio arguing over agendas and trying to fit into a format that's settled before we started the creative process is unappealing.
~ Ian Astbury

"This is not worth it" became my new mantra.

After World XXI I didn't really want to be a part of doing any original music anymore. Actually, I just about didn't want to do any music in any form.

I remember taking pads of lyrics that I wrote and tearing them up and throwing them away. I wish I'd never done that, but at that time I was angry, hurt, burned, pissed, frustrated, embarrassed. Everything was fucked up. I felt completely trampled under foot. I was back to square one. Its likely a good thing Hiro and Yasumi were across the ocean. If they'd been in New York City I would have wanted to get in their face in a not very productive or pleasant way. It was like I had been in a dating relationship and been cheated on, then dumped callously for a friend.

In more recent and calmer years I've reached out on Facebook to Hiro to talk. He's told me that he doesn't want to talk about the experience. That's all I've ever gotten out of him.

It hurt. I thought we had become friends. Were we not? Were we not even business partners at best? Was it all a game? A joke? Were they laughing at me when they got back to Japan or did they not give me another thought as they collected my publishing? Was I really just used after all? He really disappointed me, particularly as I'm sure he let Yasumi push him against his instincts. I blame her more than him for most of it, as he was just another pawn, but he had his hand in the cookie jar just the same.

It would take many years to just let it all go to where I didn't get frustrated thinking about it. Hiro and Yasumi caused me to question my whole music career and lifelong music goals.

I wanted to give up music. It was not worth it. That's how much they hurt me.

Yet, today, if he called upon the band to reunite and tour, I would do it in a heartbeat. We made some good music and I had a good experience overall. I'd put the old wounds aside to sing those songs again and really get them out there like I wanted to originally. Hiro gave me an opportunity nobody else had and I really wanted, and at a point when I was falling. I know that kinda sounds like someone who says they would go back to an ex-lover who painfully broke-up with them, against everyone's advice and their better judgment, but bands do have this strange relationship that develops. Creating art together over a period of time and the bond that develops is a strange process to describe to someone who doesn't do it. Its more than just co-workers at a normal job, as there's a sense of vulnerability.

Hiro and Yasumi hurt me so bad I didn't want to be vulnerable anymore. It wasn't worth it. I was like someone who is so hurt by a relationship they don't want to date again.

On the good side, I still talk to Dave periodically and I'm glad to still have his friendship. Did I ever think of bailing early like he did? Never, though I don't begrudge him for wanting to leave. He likely didn't see things getting better. He was proven right and avoided a lot of headaches. He got all he wanted, and more with a future wife in Rika, and left before it got worse.

Maybe I should have followed his exit, but every band has difficulties of some sort. The Canadian metal band Anvil made a movie about their international tours that were just as bad as ours, and it was one of the running gags of Spinal Tap - The Movie. I didn't see our disastrous tour as the end of the band, nor things like our publishing argument as a that much out of the ordinary. Bands much bigger than us have fought over much worse and broke up over much less, so while things were hard I thought the band could overcome it. I didn't see the writing on the wall that Dave likely saw.

Maybe Hiro and Yasumi couldn't see any light at the end of the tunnel, like I did. Maybe they weren't interested in looking for one. I saw the light. I saw what could be. I remained an optimist to the end, happy to be a part of a band making great music, even if we had our very own Yoko Ono. I always tried my hardest to make—everything work. Every time something got thrown at me I tried to fix it. I would grab whatever resources I could get to make things happen.

This is how I am about life. When I commit to something, whatever it is, its usually hard to get me out of it. Usually someone pushes themselves away from me, for whatever reason, unless I see the writing on the wall that its the Titanic I'm on. I didn't think World XXI was the Titanic, or even the Andrea Gail caught in a perfect storm. It may sound naive in hindsight, but I really didn't.

The irony is that some might propose that the signs of eventual failure were there from day one in an almost haunting way. Dave and I got off the plane and, courtesy of the management company Yasumi would come to dismiss, were brought to a hotel on the suburb of Tokyo. The rooms were entered from the outside, with the two of us on opposite sides of the building. It was dusk and the light outside my room was flickering, but none of the other lights were. I thought it was strange, as this was not the Japanese equivalent of a slum motel. I might not have thought about it again, had I not spent the next month sleeping in a room I believed to be actually haunted.

In the evenings after rehearsals I'd often grab a cheap saké from the famous Japanese vending machines on every corner and pass out asleep before long. Yet, I'd often be abruptly awaken by a presence in the room, like I wasn't welcomed there sorta vibe, while lights inside would flicker. I tried explaining to my management that I thought the room was haunted. After working for the psychic in New York I had grown more aware of mysterious energies. The management told me people would go to hotels to commit suicide.

About a week later I was woken from a saké slumber by a guy screaming. It seemed to come from the air right above the bed, continuing after I was clearly awake and not dreaming. It soon enough ended, though I had no clue what exactly I'd heard or where it was coming from, but I clearly heard something.

A couple days later I'm sitting on the bed, when it starts moving up and down vigorously. I wasn't doing anything, just sitting there. It was seriously like out of a horror movie. Given my religious upbringing I started praying and equally freaking out. Then the phone rings and its Dave from his room. "Jean, can you feel that?" Absolutely! Dave said it was an earthquake. I cried out thanking god. I heard an exasperated, "Are you out of your fucking mind?" I thought it was the devil finally come for me. I was very much freaking out until Dave told me the situation.

A couple days later management moved me out to the other side of the building near Dave. They didn't ask any more questions and told me they weren't going to talk about it anymore. I think they suspected the room was haunted, but they put me in there thinking as a foreigner I wouldn't notice anything unusual.

That was how I was introduced to life in Japan, with a haunted hotel room. It wasn't the devil coming for me, but to this day I still have no logical explanation for all that I experienced. How many hotels are legitimately haunted? Likely only a handful. Yet, against the odds I got stuck in one. The experience was a bit surreal. Some might even say it was an omen of things to come with World XXI. Maybe some spirit was trying to scare me back to America. Maybe I should blame the break-up of the band on dead spirits and not Yasumi.

The real kicker is nothing is being done with the album today. The American version didn't get sold in the U.S. and we pre-dated the digital revolution. The American label predictably had a fight with Yasumi, who was as much a nightmare to them as she was to everyone else. If the Japanese label wanted World XXI to be a real commercial success they had absolutely the wrong person commanding the ship. If she had some grand scheme of power, fame or fortune I can't really see how she succeeded on any level. I can get over the hurt friendships, but the lack of distribution and the publishing owed me are lingering frustrations.

We made a great product that I believe could definitely compete in today's market. Folks that like Five Finger Death Punch would like what we created. Folks who like Billy Sheehan would likely gravitate to Dave's bass playing, and those who only know me singing cover songs would get to hear some of my original music. 'Mechanic Beast' has one of the best ranges I've ever hit with any band. That song is also perfect for today's society, as my lyrics were ahead of their time. They talk about a beast that consumes everything, which is what social media has become, with the line, 'The only thing on TV is the beast making his rounds.'

Yet, the album masters are just sitting on a shelf somewhere and a few copies float around on the internet for the curious buyer, while Dave has put up some songs on youtube out of nostalgia. If Hiro would talk to me I'd tell him to give it a formal digital release. Though, of course, I'd like to also make some money from it this time.

8

NOBODY'S FAULT BUT MINE

It's like Samuel Beckett said: 'I can't go on, I'll go on.' Like one of those moments, where you're looking at it all and you're going, 'I can't do this anymore.' And you go, 'Well, you keep going.'
~ Ian Astbury

Hiro and Yasumi really put such a bad taste in my mouth when it came to being in a band and doing original music that I really was considering if it was worth it in the end. I kept asking myself: 'Am I gonna throw music away? It would be easy to do.' Many musicians have sold their gear and not played for years, fading into the world of 9 to 5 jobs and families and the real world. I didn't have any gear to sell and one album few had heard. It would be easy to fade away. I'd only have to deal with the bad memories, and we all have those. I had not become the MTV star I wanted to be, and I was burned badly in the failure of that dream.

Tommy Gunn, who was a major promotions guy back in the day and knew everything that had went down, put it this way to me: "Look, you got hired, you got to go to Japan, you got to be a rock star for a bit. Take it for all it was worth."

He was actually right.

Yes, it didn't work out, but I'd gotten signed to a label, lived abroad on someone else's tab, made a new friend in a great bassist and played with some great musicians, recorded an album I was proud of, improved my vocals dramatically, worked with a great producer and songwriter, and toured with iconic chart-toppers Quiet Riot, Stephen Pearcy and Carmine Appice's band. I had become the rock star I dreamed of being. It just did not last long.

Avant Garde might have made it with different timing. Naked City blew it, but our timing was also off. My solo efforts failed from internal problems that never would have worked. World XXI had a dictatorship and became a farce. My music career wasn't looking that spectacular in hindsight. But, now I began to reconsider things in light of Tommy's advice. If I threw it away now in frustration than there was nobody to blame but myself.

I'd lived the dream, now I just needed to figure out what was next, what I wanted and what was important to me. I'd actually gained more than I lost and done things others were still dreaming about. If anything had really been lost it was just a bit of money and some friends who likely weren't friends to start with.

Avant Garde had taught me the basics. Naked City had made me a hot ticket and helped me hone my craft. I got to play all the top clubs of New York City and be managed by one of its movers and shakers. World XXI had given me an album and better vocal chops. I'd got to make music my full time job for a short while. I'd done what I'd set out to do as a boy pretending to be the Beatles and Ian Astbury.

Tommy was absolutely right. Thus, I decided to take what I had and move on. The key was not to destroy my dreams, but to re-evaluate.

The secret is to figure out a way to adapt and be happy doing something new. If a dream collapses then the solution is to rework the dream, not abandon it completely. Hiro recruited me for World XXI as he saw something in me. Don and Jonathan saw something in me, too. They made my dreams come true and gave me opportunities I might not have had otherwise. The dream fell apart, but underneath the hurt I didn't actually stop dreaming. The dreams just needed to be dug out from under the rubble and brushed off.

Dreams are amazing things. I find people who follow their dreams amazing. They are truly inspiring and inspire me to not give up dreaming.

Elon Musk is one such person I find inspiring. Who dreams of taking a rocket ship to Mars and then attempts to actually make it happen, along with countless other things? He's doing it! That's amazing to me and truly inspiring.

Someone else who inspires me is Sammy Hagar. I was driving to a show in New Hampshire with a band mate and on the way we were listening to an interview of Sammy by radio host Eddie Trunk. Sammy just seems to have this great attitude about everything, and he's had some rough spots in his career. I was so inspired listening to him. He just keeps on trucking with a smile and a tequila and a continuous stream of great music. That's infectious. I will say that a few times I've had my voice compared to him, from his early Montrose days. I consider that a humbling compliment.

Inspirational in different ways are folks like Edgar Cayce and Aleister Crowley, who tried to reach new spiritual levels. While Elon is trying to find out more about the physical world, and Sammy in how to express one's self, Edgar and Aleister were trying to discover more about themselves and the spiritual world. While after discovering those mystical worlds, how could they turn that around and give something back to the world? Jimmy Page was so inspired by Aleister that he became part of the mythos surrounding Led Zeppelin.

I read a book about Edgar and found him interesting. He saw himself as having two different personalities and was nervous about his more mysterious other side. He didn't take advantage of it or make a fortune, but instead turned it to helping countless people to the present day. I think of him in terms of my born again Christian upbringing and the battles I had with my parents over things like Led Zeppelin being an evil Satanic band. I don't think they were even close to being this evil machine, much like Edgar had another side but it wasn't a Mr. Hyde, as he was tapping into something mysterious but not evil. Zeppelin made a lot of people happy with their music. Singing their music has come to make me happy. Singing is a gift I've been blessed with, and while it might seem to some that I'm doing something wrong I'm actually helping people.

Looking at my music career lying tattered at my feet, I now remembered more than anything Jonathan Love's advice of: "In order to know where you're going you always have to remember where you've been." This was what Tommy also was saying.

I loved music. I loved singing. I loved being on stage. I loved the art of it. It was my dream. But, it was time to grow up, stop beating myself up, and take personal responsibility for how the dream would move forward. Previously others had run the show and I had followed their lead. Now I would start thinking like a businessman and take more control over my music. I would be more focused and less naive.

My revived music career took me not to original music or another band, but to the world of anonymous commercial jingles and its cousin in voice-over work. They pay well and are in and out affairs with minimal hassle, wrapped up in a day or two. Michael Bolton, Barry Manilow and Robert Palmer did tons of jingles even after they had made albums as an easy way to supplement their income. While they are a pot of gold that sustains many unknown musicians who would otherwise be struggling between gigs or in poverty, like I was. They may not make one famous like a hit single does, and there's no publishing royalties, but there's also no fighting over money and struggling on the road with bad gigs. Let alone, its all very professional. One sent me home in a car service as it got to be late in the evening.

Bruce, my guitarist from the World XXI tour, landed me a singing spot on a TV commercial for Heineken beer that aired during the 2001 Grammy Awards. That's pretty cool for a guy down on his luck, though I had to buy my own beer.

Jimi Bones hooked me up with Magic Venture Studios. I was really excited about this new venture. I would do a handful of promos for things like ABC and Good Morning, America. I got to work with engineer and producer Brian McGee, who works with Jimi to this day, and whose resume includes the Rolling Stones, Meat Loaf, Cyndi Lauper, and a who's who of rock stardom.

I did have some variables working against me. Hard rock was dying and rap was coming in bigger than ever, thus there was a move away from my particular vocal style. Though, that was nothing compared to the fact I was singing alongside professionally trained Broadway singers. It was a little intimidating. As a rock singer coming in I felt like a snaggletooth.

I also had something else working against me that taught me a huge lesson. They were doing one recording that had different people walking down the street and singing. I thought I was going to be a part of it, until I got a call. I was about 30, but somebody thought I looked too old. I got pissed, but didn't say anything in the moment and let it be. After they did some filming they thought it looked too odd and wanted more folks who looked more normal. They called me back asking if I would participate after all. "I thought I wasn't your guy?" I was a bit insulted, yet at the same time I had a chip on my shoulder. I could have swallowed my pride, done the job, made some decent money for a single day's work, and likely continued to be called for jobs. Today, I would say yes. My pride caused me to mess up a blossoming opportunity that could have been very lucrative in the long term.

Doing jingles was a nice gig, but I shut the door on this one myself. Lesson learned. The loss, without doubt, was nobody's fault but mine. The music industry is very small. It doesn't seem that way, but its very common to run into the same people or someone who knows someone you know. Everyone is networked, from musicians to people on the business end, as we are all always looking for our next opportunity and next dollar. Thus, one can never burn any bridges, as the sting can be haunting for a long time, as was my loss of the jingles gig. Having enemies or people disappointed in your work can limit future opportunities. I try not to piss anyone off and get along with everyone, but that's a lesson I learned the hard way.

9

IN THE LIGHT

I could no longer hide behind the veneer of being a rock star, we didn't have that place anymore and the only thing left for me was to be real.
~ Ian Astbury

In late 1987, back when I was with Avant Garde, I got to meet guitarist Stevie Van Zandt in a club, or Little Steven as many know him. This was before he started a second career in acting as brooding mobster Silvio Dante on TV's The Sopranos. At this point he was still just a guitarist, except he was just a guitarist who had co-founded Southside Johnny & The Asbury Jukes, played with Gary U.S. Bonds and with Bruce Springsteen in both his early backing band and was the first guitarist in the E Street Band. Little Steven shares all the guitar duties with Bruce on the albums Born To Run and Born In The U.S.A.. He's iconic. He's also famous for helping and supporting lesser known musicians.

His solo group had just finished opening for U2, on their Joshua Tree Tour, at a sold out show at Pittsburgh's Three Rivers Stadium. Sitting at the bar he gave me a bit of advice I never forgot. He said, "Whatever you do, always have a back-up plan."

When it came to the New Jersey music scene Little Steven had helped develop it. So when someone like him gives some advice, there's no choice but to listen. I was ambitious and naive, but I knew I was hearing wise words from an expert, let alone a talented musician who gone through all the highs and lows found in the business. He wasn't criticizing my music or talent, but just being honest. To become successful in the music world has just as much to do with luck as it does talent, and the industry is overly fickle and heartless.

I never forgot his advice. I did what he recommended. Now more than ever.

Picking up the pieces I took to the jingle work, but for once I also had a back-up plan. I went back to pursuing my art career, but I took it way more seriously. I put it first, for a change, instead of after the music and being a rock star. Now I would say yes to art opportunities, not no. I wasn't giving up on music in the least, but I was kinda seeing the writing on the wall for making music my primary income source. There's great value in having a cushion to fall back on.

Its an unspoken secret in the rock world that a good amount of musicians have survived at times on outside non-music related incomes. Folks from Roger Daltrey to Sammy Hagar have been in such financial binds with their bands and labels that even with charting records they required outside incomes, and supposedly Billy Joel didn't make any money from his albums until the 1980's. While other musicians have chosen to have outside incomes to weather the financial pitfalls of a music career. It can also be hard to raise a family if one is going on tours where the band is barely breaking even because trends changed away from one's style.

I morphed from from being a full-time musician who did art on the side to being a full-time artist doing music on the side. For the most part, its been like that to the present day. I don't regret the decision. I honestly love my job and have done some amazing things artistically. I've had my own art business and worked for others. I would tell anyone, in the arts or not, the advice Little Steven told me. Stability, realistic hours, a steady paycheck and an environment without drinking and drugs has a lot going for it.

My first wife, who I met around this time and was strongly encouraging me to have a full-time job that likely wasn't music related, worked with a new age publishing company. I got to illustrate and design book covers for their New Age division, including some youth publications in the style of Harry Potter and a guide to J.R.R. Tolkein's literary fantasy world. I've also had my graphic design work in reports for the U.S. Congress and the White House. While clients have included the University of South Carolina, F.E.M.A., Verizon, Capital One and Toys R' Us. Ironically, many of my co-workers and clients enjoy the fact I'm in the shadow of the rock gods on the side.

10

IN MY TIME OF DYING

It seems that so many fans and bands are looking back to bands like Zeppelin because they have no better idea how to go forward.
~ Robert Plant

Even though I'd decided to keep going doing music, on some level I really was burnt on original music. Not to mention seeing so many of my friends make great music but not get any farther than I had, or even not far at all. To think about how many bands are out there and how many become Guns N' Roses makes one realize the odds are stacked against all of us no matter what we do.

Even though I was establishing my art career again and enjoyed the jingle work I was still groping around in a bit of a fog trying to figure out where I was going and where I wanted to be. Maybe it was a fool's errand, but I decided to make another attempt at doing original music. Doing my own music was so much a part of my life I couldn't break cold turkey. One might even accuse me of being a glutton for punishment, but I was thinking just one more time. Maybe if I was more in control of the variables I could have better results. This is also what addicts say, I know. Just because the last few trips were bad ones didn't mean this one would also be bad, they also say. I'll confess to being an addict to the music.

I met this lady named Aimie Kristie in New Jersey, where I was living. She was a famous radio DJ who hosted a nationally broadcast show called the Electric Ballroom featuring a lot of underground music. Her boyfriend was a bassist. One thing led to another and I proposed forming a hard rock band. Guitarist Fred Gorhau fleshed out the line-up. I named us Rattlesnake Canyon.

We ended up doing a handful of exciting shows. We opened for Vince Neil, Slaughter and Bret Michaels of Poison. We played at a strip club/nightclub in north Jersey and sorta appeared on the TV show Queer Eye For The Straight Guy.

They were bringing their client to the club. We weren't really in the show, but my brother was filmed walking out after the show saying how good we were.

I was seeking some record people to get us a deal. We even made some demos to share with anyone who would listen. We did one showcase performance, but no bites. Sorta. Somebody tried to steal Fred afterwards. For me, a showcase is about the band and not single players. Its my dime and I'm not paying people to find ways to leave my band. I know that may sound hypocritical, as I got picked out by Hiro from Naked City, but I was approached after we broke up.

Eventually, after too many arguments, Aimie broke up with and fired her boyfriend. Though, honestly, things weren't really going anywhere for the band after a year and a half. I was doing everything that I'd done in the past, and looking at the same results where success was always just around the corner. We were pretty good, but it just wasn't meant to be. It didn't help that my wife was constantly pressuring on me to find full-time and stable, let alone real, work. The band soon folded.

I was going in circles with original bands. Rattlesnake Canyon seemed to be the end of the line. No matter what happened, or what I tried or who I worked with, it all came down to really not being worth it. My motto had been right.

Just before Rattlesnake Canyon Jimi Bones and I formed Time Of Dying. Time Of Dying was something different from anything I'd done before, as it was exclusively a covers band. No originals in sight or even to be attempted. We focused on Led Zeppelin. The band was all about having fun and laughs with great music. We were doing it for the extra money with no expectations or real long-term plans. Tribute bands don't get signed to labels and make albums, so we didn't have that pressure. This was just some guys having fun with great classic songs and hopefully it was contagious with the audience. End of story. Thus, the band was a very different, let alone refreshing, gig from my past outings.

The idea for a tribute band we actually put in the air before World XXI folded. Now it seemed like a good way to help get the ground firmly back under my feet, and the time was right for both of us to play together again. It was also a good way to branch out into sounds I might not do on my own. Everybody seems to like Led Zeppelin, whatever their other musical tastes, so I could also reach out to an audience I would never get otherwise.

Time Of Dying was officially born at the Rock'N'Roll Cafe, which also happened to be where I met my first wife who was working the bar. We played there nearly every month. They had a lot of tribute bands and it was a good home. Clubs generally welcome cover bands and book them frequently, as they usually fill the club which translates to more sales at the bar. Even bad cover bands can often get an audience in, while original groups can struggle if they don't have a reputation outside of friends. Next door to the Cafe was Kenny's Castaways were we also played periodically. Before its closure in 2012 this was a place to be seen. I remember seeing actors, musicians and even local politicians hanging out there.

Aside from playing in Skin N' Bones and Kix, Jimi would play guitar and an array of instruments for a lot of TV shows, like <u>Double Dare</u>, <u>The View</u>, <u>The Price Is Right</u>, and has worked with bands such as Katrina And The Waves, the Jonas Brothers, Blondie and Joan Jett. Not just has he been a supportive friend, but he's one of the best guitarists I've worked with. He's a natural. He reminds me of Slash's playing in Guns N' Roses. He would make that guitar sing and make Jimmy Page's classic Zeppelin riffs look like child's play. I don't think there was anything he couldn't play.

Numerous musicians came through the ranks of Time Of Dying. Aaron A. Brooks, also known as Aaron Kinsley-Brooks, was our drummer for awhile. He's a killer drummer and has played with Moby, Jim Croce's piano playing son A.J., and Duff McKagan of Guns N' Roses, and would form a band with our keyboardist Joe called Baldwin Drive. Another time we had behind us on drums John Miceli, whose resume would include Meat Loaf and My Chemical Romance. He is one of the best drummers I've ever played with. Another time we had Thommy Price sit in on drums for a show. The guy has played with Billy Idol, Joan Jett, Roger Daltrey, Ronnie Wood and tons of others. I was pretty stoked, until he didn't get the songs right during the gig. He didn't put an effort into learning the songs. He tried to fake Zeppelin, but the songs are too unique and many in the audience have them memorized. I didn't push it with him, but I wasn't happy. We may have only done the band for fun, but that didn't mean we weren't serious about the music. On the other hand, I guess at least I can brag about who I've played with.

Between our built-in audience and Jimi's connections we got to play Madison Square Garden four or five times, where we expanded our set to include bands like Metallica. Jimi had worked out a deal where we were the house band for the arena football team the New York CityHawks. One of my bandmates, keyboardist Joe "Pajamas" Chiofalo, wrote the anthem for the team which we performed. Yes, I can say I've played Led Zeppelin at the Garden. Though, honestly, nobody was really there to hear us. As people were coming into the Garden we'd play and then during some breaks. Joe likes to say they came for the game, but ended up enjoying us better. I don't know if that's true, but the team only lasted a year before leaving town and eventually folded. I remember the rival team, the New Jersey Devil Dogs or something like that, were throwing ice cubes at us. I remember one bouncing off my drummer's snare drum. The trials of live gigs at football games.

Singing Robert Plant's iconic lyrics might seem intimidating to some, particularly at the Garden with thousands in attendance, but World XXI had put me through the paces and made me a stronger singer able to tackle such a challenge. I had a lot of confidence in myself. I didn't feel like there was anything I couldn't sing, plus I'd already done lots of covers with Avant Garde with other bands that posed their own set of musical challenges. This might be a bit arrogant, but it meant Time Of Dying came out the door gangbusters.

Further, the audiences seemed to be enjoying it as much as we were. I remember at Kenny's Castaways a group of West Point cadets who would regularly come see us. It started as a few and then the group grew bigger. One of the guys met a girl there who he later married. I saw him after he graduated and he told me, "I never would have met the girl of my dreams if it wasn't for you." He gifted me a t-shirt and his Challenge Coin in thanks.

Being compared to Sammy Hagar is one thing, but thanked for changing someone's life is unimaginable. His words make me feel like there's a reason for what I'm doing. It makes it all worth while. To think I almost didn't do music again. Comments like his verified I'd taken the right path.

11

IN THE EVENING

So you grow into the person that you didn't know you were going to be.
~ Robert Plant

People were really enjoying what we were doing with Time Of Dying and I was enjoying the music. Honestly, it took me a little by surprise given what I'd previously been through and struggled with. I saw the fun I was having. I saw the great response we were getting. I loved watching the energy of the band pass back and forth from the crowd, where its not about me or any of us, but just a great experience for everyone at the show. More importantly, I saw the potential of what this Led Zeppelin thing could be. A golden opportunity had potentially landed in my lap from a source I least expected.

I decided I wanted to try to take Time Of Dying to a bigger level and reach wider audiences. I didn't just want to play clubs in New York City anymore to small audiences or at football games where nobody came for the music. I wanted to play theaters and festivals and keep branching out, cross the river to New Jersey and then head to Maryland and Pennsylvania and beyond. My goal became to take the show on the road as far as I could and see where I could take this. I was looking at what other tribute bands were doing. Fellow Zeppelin tribute band Get The Led Out was one of the first tribute bands that broke into the theater scene. Another Zeppelin tribute band that had done theaters was Florida based Physical Graffiti. These were the models for what I thought we could achieve.

Sadly, I saw the guys who I was playing with just weren't going to be able to take the next step with me. They were all busy session guys or had other tour obligations. Thus, in 2000 I turned Time Of Dying into Kashmir and slowly brought in a new team of players and built up a steady calendar of shows moving beyond the club scene. Since it was my primary gig by default it became my baby. I would be more in control on this musical adventure than I had been in the past. Professionalism was the modus operandi.

I've come to really like playing theaters and festivals, so hindsight has shown the move was the right one. Let alone Kashmir has now surpassed twenty years. I'm the only original member left, but my guitarist, Andy Urban, has been with me since 2003. I think its fair to say, with Kashmir I finally got all the right pieces in play. It may not be the music career I dreamed about as a boy with the MTV videos and albums, but I love what I do and the music we make. Its not always been a breeze and there's been hurdles and learning moments, but its worked the way nothing else has. Had I not been open to trying new things I don't know if I'd be as successful in music as I've become.

I'm also making more money than with previous bands and doing it without an album or label or hit single. Its interesting how things work out. The funny part is, when I first started in music, my original hair color was dark brown, but as I played and the years went on, I started to lighten it. I slowly progressed to becoming fully blonde. I always tell people, kidding around, the blonder my hair, the more money I make.

In the first few years Kashmir busted my ass. We played over 100 shows a year. It was burn-out level, but it really established us on the scene. Now I have a more sustainable schedule and is what is called a weekend warrior. Instead of going out for months at a time, the band goes out for the equivalent of a long weekend or for just a night. We may fly in for a gig, but one of us is likely driving the trailer with the equipment, so most gigs are East Coast oriented where we all live. Kashmir is not a full-time job for any of us. I have a day job that expects me Monday morning unless I take vacation time and being a rock star is not an excuse to miss work unexcused.

I sometimes get asked if anyone from Led Zeppelin or their greater business entity has ever reached out to any of us or given us a stamp of approval. Nope. I've met folks active in the band's fan scene, like memorabilia collectors, who have met members of the band and associated people, but that's as close as I've gotten. The remaining band members may not even know Kashmir exists. Jimmy Page sometimes mentions in interviews some tribute and covers bands he has come across, but I don't know how much the Zeppelin guys actually pay attention to all of us out here playing their music and being them on stage. I've not reached out to them either. Maybe my bassist, Felix Hanneman, might have met the guys, as he's been making music since the '70's, but that would have been long before Kashmir.

I will say that in 2019 Rolling Stone magazine did a collectors edition issue dedicated to the 50 opening paragraph of the lead article reads: "More than three decades after the end of Led Zeppelin, they are everywhere. They've sold nearly 25 million albums since 1990 alone, and every night bands with names like Kashmir, No Quarter and Lez Zeppelin cover their songs in bars and clubs worldwide." Now if the guys read the article, then I can say they have heard of us.

If I did chance to meet Jimmy, Robert or John Paul, what might I say to them given I have over twenty years under my belt being Robert Plant on stage? Truthfully, I would probably just walk up and shake their hand and thank them. Thank them for writing such great music. What more can really be said for a band whose influence on music cannot be measured, and whose music continues to influence the world decades after the band ceased? They provided this musical source to tap into to take away peoples' troubles and take them to another place in time. Words cannot describe their contribution to the world, musical or otherwise. Then I might ask them if they actually did record stuff backwards on 'Stairway To Heaven'? If they did its sorta amazing if the rumors are true.

I don't know if I would ask Robert for advice. When I see interviews with him he seems to be friendly, but to a point. I don't know how happy he is about people being him on stage. While his own solo music has gone far beyond anything Led Zeppelin did into something very different, with his recent forays into acoustic and folk music. Really, I'd rather not have something bad happen with the interaction, so I'd probably just say thank you for the music.

I have met other rock stars. I've met Bret Michaels of Poison, Vince Neil of Mötley Crüe and Canadian rock guitarist Pat Travers. Travers' bassist Charlie Torres is a friend, who has also played with Edgar Winters and Chuck Berry. I've got to hang out with and meet members of REO Speedwagon, Great White, Lynyrd Skynyrd, the Doobie Brothers and Kiss. Don

Felder of the Eagles, who wrote the music for 'Hotel California', was super nice when I met him.

I would also cross paths again with Carmine Appice, following our tour together in Japan. I had lunch with him and we hashed out a plan where he would play a set with Kashmir. He'd also tell stories on stage, and there would be a meet-and-greet. It would be historic because Zeppelin's first tour was with Carmine's band Vanilla Fudge. Sadly, we never got beyond the talking stages for something that would have been cool.

I will be honest in that meeting stars is not always the most glamorous thing. Not every encounter is like sitting at the bar with Little Steven. Even though I'm a frontman, I'm actually a bit shy off stage, so I tend to be reserved approaching someone to talk even if we're backstage together. These stars are just people. Some are social and some are not. While I know I'm not a superstar who everyone is waiting to meet.

I find a lot of lesser known and younger musicians have huge heads and think they are as great as sliced bread. They can be a bit stand-offish. They won't allow us in the dressing area or at the food buffet or have areas where nobody is allowed, even though we're on the bill with them. I wonder if they have forgotten when they were just a struggling opening act? Perhaps they think this is the way super rock stars are supposed to act. To which I give the example of when a member of a reunited Autograph looked down on us and banned us from being around them at a festival. They are largely a one hit wonder from 1984, with only 3 charting hits in the States. Yet, while they were too good for us I was backstage hanging out with the keyboardist of Lynyrd Skynyrd, a band with 19 charting hits in the U.S. including one spawning the jokey phrase "Play 'Free Bird'" heard regularly at concerts of every type.

To the disappointment of many up-and-coming bands on tour who are looking forward to meeting their heroes, all of us are not necessarily hanging out backstage like old friends. Sometimes we might and other times we might be banned, but sometimes logistics mean we don't actually cross paths. I've had shows where I've never met the other bands gracing the stage with us due to the different show times. This is particularly true with festivals spread out over many hours where bands are coming and going and not necessarily staying to socialize. By the time we do our gig a band going on later might not have even arrived yet, and we might have to get on the road so we neither see nor meet them. With World XXI I often saw Quiet Riot from the audience just like everyone else and that was all the interaction I had with them that night.

I was backstage at a Ted Nugent show a few years ago with my son-in-law. His bassist at the time, Greg Smith, is a friend. He is now playing with my old bandmate Fred Gorhau in Wizards of Winter. I've always liked Ted's music and he's so self-assured on stage. Whatever one may think of his politics, his love for the music shines on stage. He owns the audience like all the great frontmen I've admired. My son-in-law was a fan and we wanted him to sign our t-shirt. At the right side of the stage were only the technicians and us other musicians. Sadly, this was one of the times that Ted had said something in the media and death threats had come his way. As soon as the show was over he exited stage left. He was immediately surrounded by his security and went directly into the van and was gone. We were told he was afraid, but this is a guy that has guns with him all the time. Couldn't he have taken a few minutes to say hi to the opening bands on the other side of the stage that were in his view from the stage and obviously not dangerous? I was pretty disappointed by that.

Then there's times when maybe I wish I hadn't met someone. During my Naked City days Don Hill used to have these local jams and was doing a tribute night to Joey Ramone. Peter Steele, the vocalist and bassist of metal band Type O Negative, was going to play with us. Before the show he got caught up in the celebration and ended up totally wasted. As he was walking up the stage stairs he fell flat on his face. He got up and tried to join us, but after a few minutes we had to get him off the stage for his own safety and everyone's embarrassment. He would struggle with addiction all his life, and get sober before a too early death.

During those same days everyone used to go to the Scrap Bar on MacDougal Street after their gigs. I met there the late vocalist Ray Gillen of Badlands and Black Sabbath. I was a big fan, but he was really aloof and not too nice. Its hard to really know what's going on the minds of some of these stars.

12

BOOGIE WITH STU

We're still kids at heart, we love playing live, and when we lock in, we throw down. We want to ignite imaginations. Hopefully everyone will leave exhausted, exhilarated, energized and inspired.
~ Ian Astbury

I've had about a dozen guys come through Kashmir. All talented players.
Originally we were a quintet with a keyboardist, but I wanted to go higher and get more like Led Zeppelin. Get The Led Out is a tribute band that tries for the exact sound with two guitarists, but doesn't attempt the look. I really wanted to get the look and an authentic live experience. I changed us to a quartet with a bassist who also plays keyboards and mandolin, just like John Paul Jones did when the band played live.

Since 2006 my drummer has been Paul Cooper, who actually looks a lot like Roger Waters from Pink Floyd. Audiences love it when he goes into John Bonham's famous drum solo 'Moby Dick'. He's the only one I know who plays the solo with the back of his hands. I don't know why his knuckles haven't fallen off mid-solo. He has a background playing jazz and funk and even played on the Bob Hope Show. Yet, he's also very loyal and not one of the mercenaries I don't like. Having that loyalty and dependability is more important than someone who can play exactly like Bonham. Besides the fact there's really only one Bonham, skills can be developed over time, but not necessarily loyalty. When Paul auditioned for us there was another drummer we also tried out. The other guy was really really good, but Paul had the loyalty factor.
I also made Paul our road manager. He's a great communicator who networks well and really likes the business side of music. For awhile he was trying to be an agent and was working with a couple bands. He likes that type of interaction,

which I absolutely despise and can't do as well as him. He takes a lot of stress off my shoulders.

In Paul I got a two-fer I never expected. I should have seen it from the beginning as we immediately fused both in personality and playing together. He's like me in that he will use every resource he has available for the band. I have to remind him not to use his van at his own expense, as the band budget will cover things. Yet, complaining about someone spending their own money versus some of the things I've encountered in other bands makes it hardly a complaint worth mentioning.

Actually, he's a three-fer. When Kashmir first started I was moving the trailers with the gear, but my trucks always had something go wrong in the process, like having the break line blow on my way home from a gig. In about two years I put 130,000 miles on my still brand new truck. I began to feel like I was doing too much. Paul took over hauling the trailer and the band budget covers him. Even more stress off my shoulders.

I had an earlier drummer who had issues with traveling after getting into an accident with another band. Thus, I'm blessed having found Paul to fill the drum chair, plus some.

I also had a drummer named Brian. He met a girl and got married. He could no longer give the band the same level of commitment. He gave us fair warning and stayed till we could find a replacement, which was Paul. I was sad to see him go, but happy he had a new adventure ahead of him.

On guitar is Andy Urban, whose been playing Jimmy to my Robert since 2003. Andy is a big Zeppelin fan. He seems to always be finding obscure recordings and can talk for hours on their history and music. He's the collector and history buff that I'm not. He's played in a bunch of other cover bands, including one doing AC/DC. He was previously in a Zeppelin tribute band that broke up. He went looking for another when he saw my ad. I warned him at our first rehearsal to be prepared for a roller coaster. He hasn't gotten off the ride yet, thankfully.

He's a very good guitarist. He's also very loyal and committed. I don't know if Kashmir would be the band it is, let alone still be around, if I was always going through musicians. The fact he eventually learned to play the theremin, just like Jimmy did, shows his commitment to getting the authentic Zeppelin live experience and sound. He also pulls out the bow to properly do the solo of 'Whole Lotta Love.' One of the things he does really well is getting those proper tones with the right equipment. Sometimes he shocks me by how much he sounds just like Jimmy. He's really into capturing that exact sound and not just do I like it, but our audience loves it.

He also has captured Jimmy's very unique body movements, which includes a lot quirky leg movements like some odd English country jig. I like to say Jimmy and Andy are off-time. I'll hear Andy playing in time, but he'll stomp off-time and sometimes it'll mess me up.

Before Andy, I had Fred Gorhau, who was simultaneously playing with me in Rattlesnake Canyon. He left Kashmir to focus more on his kids and day job. Today he plays in Wizards Of Winter. They started as a tribute band to Trans-Siberian Orchestra before doing their own music exclusively. They are a success story like Kashmir, as they moved from local gigs to national tours when they saw the potential, while they have had ex-members of Trans-Siberian Orchestra join their ranks. The world of tribute bands is an amazing world that has blessed many of us with unexpected second careers.

On bass, keyboards and mandolin is Felix Hanemann. He is a founding member of the 1970's rock band Zebra with guitarist Randy Jackson and drummer Guy Gelso. His inclusion is unintentionally ironic, as Zebra started out as a covers band doing Led Zeppelin and other prog rock bands before recording their own songs. They were even hailed as filling the void when Zeppelin disbanded. Felix was also in Hindenberg, another Zeppelin tribute band with members of Ace Frehley's band, but he left after it created numerous conflicts with Kashmir. Felix has also played with Rainbow and Deep Purple frontman Joe Lynn Turner and Yngwie Malmsteen bassist Randy Coven.

At one point I had a different player on keyboards, bass and mandolin. Like me, this fellow had also spent the '90's in New York City playing all the clubs before finding a second successful career in the tribute band scene. His departure ended up being a moment where I had it dramatically re-affirmed why I don't want to be surrounded by people drunk and high.

He had gotten a new girlfriend. Everyone knew very quickly that the writing was on the wall when it came to his future with the band, to the point where we were thinking about his replacement. Everyone that is, except for him. At one gig we watched from the stage as the club owner went from talking and drinking with the girlfriend to vanishing with her to the basement. They didn't re-appear until our set was over. None of us knew what was down there and the club's staff confessed to not knowing what was going on. It didn't look good to anyone, except to her oblivious boyfriend. There had been other questionable situations like this, while other times she'd just be drunk and acting crazy.

    I eventually called my bassist to confront him about the situation. He wasn't a bad guy, but had introduced a bad element into the fold. I told him straight that she was manipulating him and was bad news. This might seem rude, but she was effecting his performance and potentially making us look bad. What club wants to re-hire a band with questionable girlfriends that might cause trouble? Or, what band wants to work in a club that is just interested in sneaking away with a band member's girlfriend? What neither of us knew was that while I was telling him what an asshole his girlfriend is, she was on the other line secretly listening. She soon made her presence known. Our working relationship and friendship died after that phone call, as could be expected.

    Kashmir did a show in Colonial Beach, Virginia where the pair started drinking a lot. We had two shows that night, so I warned him about pacing himself as there was five hours to go. No surprise they were both hammered by the time we went on. She made a big scene, including getting on stage with her camera. I don't like people getting on stage with us, as things can get damaged, let alone they just get in our way. Paul and I asked her to get off, but she didn't listen. I eventually screamed at her to leave, but still nothing happened. Over the microphone I called security and had her kicked off the premises. After the show she was found outside having a breakdown and kicking my truck, to the point where I was talking to the police. Earlier, when I had her removed her my bassist resigned right on stage in protest. Audiences don't pay to see a band breakdown. That is not part of the live Led Zeppelin experience by any factor. We're not a Guns N' Roses tribute band.

    While this was going on Paul had gotten on a phone backstage and called Felix. Paul had approached him earlier about doing a few shows on a substitute basis, but now we needed him ASAP for all the shows. I didn't know Felix too well, but Paul knew him from the Upper Westchester music scene. Paul had worked at Atlantic Records doing some back-up session work and met and played with Felix there, so now I would have a rhythm section with a built-in camaraderie. The fact Felix had already played the songs was just a bonus at this point.

    Matt Stanley is our unofficial fifth man. He steps in when Felix has obligations keeping him from a performance. He's an incredible musician, especially on mandolin. We met when I was at a New Jersey unemployment agency. I was talking to this nice woman who worked there and told her I was a musician. She said her son played keyboards. Ironically, at that time I was looking for a keyboardist. She gave me his number. He played with us steady until he got married and became a family man.

    When we were a quintet I had Frank on bass and Rob on keyboards. I really wanted to get closer to the authentic live sound. This isn't possible when there's both a keyboardist and bassist playing simultaneously, which Zeppelin never did outside the studio. I told Frank I loved having him in the band, but Rob could also play bass, so it made sense to have him take up both instruments.

    This transition was something I thought about and didn't just make hastily overnight. It came about as I saw not downsizing would be a detriment to the band's growth. Something wasn't quite working out on stage visually. Attempts to fix it with the guys wasn't making a difference. I always give people room to help me fix problems, as we're all in this together, but some people don't always share my goals. The light bulb moment came when after a couple years playing a festival in Akron, we were turned down and the Led Zeppelin tribute band Zoso took our spot. It became undeniably obvious that we weren't doing what we should be doing on stage. I don't want that to happen again.

    Being surrounded by such talented players I've been asked if Kashmir has ever thought of doing our own music, if even on the side. Its has never really come up. Its like we all get together to play Led Zeppelin and somehow don't even think about doing anything else. If we do think about it, then it doesn't get mentioned. Its a very organic thing just keeping our eyes on Zeppelin. The drive to make original music just doesn't happen in our situation for unexplained reasons. It actually makes things uncomplicated, as we have enough to keep us busy.

As for recording our own album of Zeppelin covers, we'll never do that. For a royalty fee we could, but I don't see the point. We're not going to record the songs as well as the originals.

Yet, Kashmir would not be as successful as it is without some unseen faces who put in just as much hard work, but get none of the accolades and attention. Touring with us is a sound engineer, David Krol, and his assistant, Erik Davey. Eric approached David about being an apprentice and he worked out so well that I increased his duties to being our unofficial roadie. We don't have any other crew. My guys joke that I'm the only vocalist they know who loads gear into the truck. Though, Felix has friends and followers from Zebra who will often show up and help load and tune guitars. A guitar tech is on my bucket list.

David is also a keyboardist, who I met in another music project where he got to hear horror stories of my sound guy. He offered to help us out by coming into the role. He is really smart and made immediate improvements. I tend to hire people who come to me rather than seek out people. This way I get people who are truly interested in being a part of this experience, let alone have a personal interest in the results. Trying to make people interested, I learned in my brief solo career, quite often doesn't work out.

There's one more unseen face in our agent. I've worked with many agents. Some are great and some are adequate. Getting a good agent is important for a band. A bad agent doesn't necessarily see beyond the next gig or doing what is best for the successful growth of the band. A bad agent can hold the band's growth back, intentionally or not.

Before my current agent I was working with a guy who was looking to make more money for himself. His priority was not Kashmir. I wanted someone who was hungry like I was to move to the next level, but he didn't see things in the same way and was working for his own benefit usually. The breaking point was after a successful show in Plymouth, Rhode Island where he wanted us to return to the venue on a double billing with the

Zeppelin tribute band Zoso. Two bands doing the same songs in the same show is not a good idea. It might have been a big ticket seller on paper, but in practice it would have made us all look like fools and created a sense of competition I don't want to be a part of. We were still doing clubs and I wanted to break into the theater scene, not play the same venues with a band that was competing for the same gigs.

Good managers can be as hard to find as good musicians. Avant Garde always tucked away a percentage of money from every gig to cover some band expenses. On our first trip to play CBGB's I suggested the band funds cover the trip, particularly as I didn't have a full-time job and a lot of money. Our manager, who was not joining us, disagreed and fought my idea. On our second trip he came with us and immediately approved using the savings to cover all the travel expenses. It was all about his benefit and, like my Kashmir agent, he didn't put the band first. That's not a good equation.

My current agents are Sean Gilday and Rachel Hill of Blue Raven Artist out of New Jersey. Sean approached me with offers for occasional gigs going in the direction I wanted the band to take, but I was hesitant. His agency was relatively new, but eventually I saw where he lacked in a resume he made up for by being good on his offers. Eventually he became our agent and gave us a game plan on how to grow. He wanted a website, promotional videos and some other tools that he could use to properly sell us. He also came to us with sacrifices. He wanted us to cut some gigs. The theaters and festivals communicate with each other and know what bands cost and what tickets sell for. If we charge a theater or festival double or more what a bar pays that could go through the grapevine and hurt us. Thus, we had to cut the clubs from our schedule and not take every gig that came our way, but only the gigs we wanted our future to be full of. It was a plan that met a lot of hesitancy, but eventually showed its value. Now we only do a few clubs. Our agency also has a large and successful roster of bands from original chart-toppers, including Felix and Zebra, to numerous tribute bands. Ironically, one of our agency mates is the Smithereens, the first national band I ever opened for. How things come around.

13

WE'RE GONNA GROOVE

Learn to use a camera. Get good at how you image yourself and present yourself to the world. We see something now, before we hear it.
~ Ian Astbury

When I first started doing Kashmir people would call me Mr. Plant. We got treated like we were actually Led Zeppelin. There might not be any private jets, but we'd get the red carpet just the same. I didn't make it as a solo artist or in an original rock band, but I sure as hell get treated pretty close to it, and better, sometimes. Yet, at the end of the day I'm just Jean Violet, not trying to be Robert Plant. Though, at the end of the day I wish I had his bank account.

I don't try to be Robert or imitate him. I don't do his accent. Yet, I do try to emulate his mannerisms and look the best I can. He's very macho, but has this very feminine quality with the famous tied blouse and tight pants. We get a lot of kids that want to see us, as they love Zeppelin and want to hear the songs live. They look at me the way people look at Robert, I'm sure. The more I act and look like him the more it benefits the audience, and in turn the band.

I've actually been mistaken as Robert off stage. Though, he is over six feet tall and I'm only 5'7", so I'm a Mini-Me Robert. It doesn't happen so much now as he's grown older, but not everyone knows what musicians look like present day. I went to Niagara Falls about two years ago and some tourists thought I was him.

Looks aside, if folks in our audiences close their eyes it feels like they're at a Zeppelin concert. When we all hit that sweet musical spot where the four of us go into what I call the zone and the audience is with us, time just stops. That's what I want to achieve at every show. I've had audience members in their 50's and 60's saying, "I thought I was back in the '70s. That's the closest I'll ever get to seeing live Zeppelin." That's the greatest compliment. I want everyone to get their money's worth and be transported back in time. All of us in the band feel that way.

Every tribute band has a niche and ours is the live experience. We aim to try to sound the way Zeppelin did live, which doesn't always sound the same as the studio albums with their many overdubs. We go off into little jams like they did. I throw in Robert's vocal nuances that aren't heard on the studio versions. We have lights, lasers and all the different dynamics that would have been seen at one of their shows.

It really means something to me when someone older is at the show with their kids and even grand-kids, which happens a lot. Playing in festivals and theaters lets us share with every generation, which doesn't happen in clubs and one reason I wanted to grow beyond them. I see it all the time at festivals where the kids will be up front, their parents farther back and then the grandparents all the way back. They are all having the same great experience with the same music, either re-living the past or discovering new music. I love to feel that energy, take it and give it back.

Of course, not everyone goes away from our shows satisfied.

I try to be nice, but sometimes I have to bite my tongue with some of our critics. One woman sent me a really long email telling me how Felix was out of time. He's in a band called Zebra who have double platinum albums, and you are who? I likely would have noticed if he was badly out of time, given how many years we have performed these songs together. Not to mention how Naked City collapsed due to being out of time, so I know what that feels like.

I find a particular breed of musician can be my roughest critic. I swear some musicians go out of their way to express their concerns or opinions on who isn't performing to their standards. I want to tell them to just stay at home if they know they're not going to enjoy it. On some level, I appreciate sometimes someone telling me we weren't up to par and how, but others can take criticism to a really low almost personal level. One musician told me we needed to rehearse more with details why. I got really upset and figured I'd show him by rehearsing harder and getting better. Ironically, that's what he wanted. I think he showed me.

One guy wrote a three page essay on all the things we did wrong in one show. I was criticized for holding the mic with the wrong hand. I actually don't know which hand Robert holds the mic in. While Paul wasn't wearing overalls like Bonham. This audience member obviously didn't understand we're not out to duplicate Zeppelin exactly down to the detail, like the Dark Star Orchestra duplicates the Grateful Dead's concerts. We are here to keep their spirit alive and honor a live experience from the past and, more importantly, play some great classic music. We're honest about saying we may not be note for note perfect and might put a bit of ourselves into it. We try our best, but there's really only one Robert Plant, Jimmy Page, John Paul Jones and John Bonham.

To me, one of the greatest things about the Led Zeppelin's live experience is its ability to make the problems of the day be forgotten. Everything that is going on in the outside world stops for a few hours. That's what we hope Kashmir will do for everyone. If we can help our audience forget the world for a few hours than we've achieved our goal and honored their legacy. I'm not in a contest with anyone on who can be the best Robert Plant imitator.

I do try my best to do the best Robert Plant I can, with or without critics telling me what I'm doing wrong. I know that I can't be anywhere but on my game in this line of work.

I have to keep on top of things vocally. I go back to listen to stuff all the time. I might have been singing these songs for over two decades, but its natural to change them unintentionally or get into bad habits that I don't realize I'm doing until I hear the recordings again. I'm always catching myself singing too hard or modulating to a higher key. Robert's vocals were great and powerful, but he's really not working that hard. He wasn't forcing it, which is one reason he always sounds so good live, and still has a strong voice decades later. He didn't push himself and ruin his voice. I don't want to ruin mine, and thus have to continuously be aware of what I'm doing. Being on my game means hitting the right notes and taking care of my voice. Many of his peers are examples of doing it the wrong way and have hurt their vocal cords, which are already impacted by aging. We regularly switch up our set list, and that's a great time to go back and double check how I'm doing.

My wife says that while I do Robert really well I don't sound like an imitator just running through the songs and unable to sing anything else. My singing has soul to it. I credit that to training all these years. Not just do I learn the songs, but I also regularly practice my scales and general intonation, which got started with World XXI. Modern technology offers a lot of applications to help this process. There's a vocal coach on youtube named Eric Arceneaux who works with singers, including Broadway performers, in ways I've found very helpful. He teaches things like working on scales, breathing techniques, warming up with weird noises instead of lyrics, learning to open the whole throat using both science and Eastern breathing practices usually found in spiritual circles. Sometimes I have to practice his stuff in the bathroom as I sound like Linda Blair in The Exorcist. One thing I do when I'm just working on my vocals in general is avoid singing Zeppelin songs. I'll work on other things, either songs by others or just sounds. This way I can regularly come to Zeppelin fresh and be aware of any bad vocal habits I might have fallen into. By taking my lessons and applying them to Zeppelin, instead of molding them to Zeppelin, I'm always rediscovering the music on some level.

I also understand my head versus my chest voice better than I did in my youth, and how to get the power I need without stretching or forcing it. I had a sound guy tell me once that I didn't have to scream into the mic. His job was to get me the volume I wanted. I just had to worry about hitting the right note and giving him something he'd want to push the volume on. I've thus learned how to focus my energy better.

I also use little things like in-ear monitors. They help a lot, particularly as I've had some hearing damage after all these decades of playing between on-stage monitors on one side of me and loud amps on the other. People who aren't performers don't understand the physical wear and tear being on a stage regularly puts on the body. Its very common to hear about drummer's with back problems, or guitarists with shoulder problems, or knee problems for everyone. I try to take the preventative medicine approach the best I can.

As I've gotten older I really see the value of rehearsing in a way I didn't when I was young. Its not just to make the music sound good, but to keep the instrument in good working order. When I was younger it was no problem to jump right on stage from whatever I was doing. It was balls to the wall. Press the on button and go. Now I've got to warm up for a half hour. Sometimes I won't even talk to anyone to conserve my voice. I think I've really learned how to pace myself with Kashmir. I also make sure I exercise, work out and diet, along with taking care of my voice. I wonder if I had done all this when I was young what effect it might have had on my singing career? If I want to be on the top of my game then I can't sit on my ass and just leave my performance up to luck.

There is also the situation where certain songs, no matter how I prepare, put a heavier demand on my voice. Some songs require a lot out of me and I have to rest my voice between gigs. I may not be able to do a particular song on multiple gigs in a row as it takes too much out of me the first night. There's also songs that I can repeat night after night, but they have a particular place in the set. A song that is going to push me a lot might be near the end of the night. If it disrupts my voice then very little of the remaining night will be ruined. While other songs are better to open with, as they allow me to slide into the night versus coming on too strong and burning out early. I've seen many singers not aware of the structure of the set in regards to their voice and end a show hoarse. Singers have to know the limits of their instrument if they want to maintain the same quality performance all night across all the songs. We've played two to three shows a week, which might include two sets in a night stretching over a couple hours. Clubs won't want us back if the second set has me hoarse, or if I show up at a gig hoarse from the night before. There are also songs that let me gauge the night. If I pull them off then I know the rest of the night will be fine. While I also deliberately plan vocal breaks, where I can rest backstage and drink some coconut water, like when Paul does the drum solo 'Moby Dick.' That's a great song to put before or after a vocally challenging one. Even a few minute guitar solo can be good.

There's no partying with Kashmir. Its all discipline and work. Its fun, but its work. When I was young I would party, then sing and then party some more. I don't do that with Kashmir. I also quite literally can't. My body can't do that like it once did, but more importantly, all of us have jobs and families and other obligations. It doesn't matter how good the Sunday night gig was, we've got work on Monday morning. None of us can get drunk and sleep until the afternoon. We have partners who will make sure of that. Now I'm often in a hotel chilling before and after gigs. It's not necessarily exciting nor glamorous, but it means I'll put in the best performance I can. That's the only thing that matters. This is my job and I take it seriously, and I want the best product I can create.

I don't have any tolerance anymore for anyone on my team who comes to a gig or rehearsal high or stoned or drunk, which obviously also includes their girlfriends and wives. That's become a pet peeve now. It goes hand in hand with my refusal to babysit, like I did in my solo outing. It's my dime, so I'm looking for a certain outcome of a certain standard. Nothing is going to be achieved when one is wasted. Some of the guys I've had in Kashmir don't even drink anymore. We've all moved beyond the party thing and learned better. Seeing many older musicians continue long past when they've had chart hits, I've found nearly universally the sober and clean ones are the ones that make it. The others made it, too, but there always came a wall they crashed against, and rarely in a pleasant way.

World XXI was were I solidified this perspective. That was a literal sobering experience because everything was completely professional. I had to be places at certain times and do certain things. There were deadlines and people counting on me. I was literally under contract and liable if I didn't pull my weight. There was no blowing off rehearsals cause I was too hungover on cheap saké. It was a very good wake-up call. I'm glad that was my wake-up call and not crashing back to earth in a hospital or jail. I don't deny there's been some great music made my musicians tanked out of their minds, like the Grateful Dead and Jim Morrison, but more often than not I've founding those moments are in the minority. The stories conveniently don't talk about all the times Jim was too wasted to do anything.

One of the most important things I've learned, outside of taking care of my instrument, is to trust people and not micro-manage everything. It's important to be surrounded with people who are good at their jobs, strive to do their best, and want everyone to succeed and not just themselves. From there its just a matter of trusting them and letting them fly. When I was younger I didn't trust people so much. Sometimes rightly so, but other times it was just because I was too full of myself and needed to be in control. Yet, it meant I was always worried about what others were doing. I couldn't focus on what I needed to do to be creative and at my best, while sitting on their shoulders didn't do them any favors either. Its impossible to get the best of people when hounding and not trusting them.

For example, I've had a great soundman the last few years in David. I trust him and he makes the band sound great, and finds ways for us to sound better. It doesn't hurt that he's the keyboardist in Classic Journey Live, so he has firsthand experience playing in a tribute band. He's open about the fact he has Asperger's, but he's found a way to let it be an asset and not a hurdle. David will place a camera on the soundboard with a good microphone and record our shows. He'll take that back to the hotel or home with him and listen to it over and over and over in a way that would drive me crazy. Then he'll come to me with suggestions, like to hold the microphone closer. David can hear things I would never hear in a recording. He'll then record again with the change and we'll compare both recordings. The improvement will be noticeable. With his assistant, Erik, he'll talk about decibels and gear and things that as the singer dude I don't really know about. All I know is I trust him and he never lets me or the band down.

Kashmir is my band, but I do try to make it more of a democracy when it comes to decisions. This is where being surrounded by good people is necessary, as I know they have the band's interest at heart, not just their own. Yet, when push comes to shove I'll use the singer trump card. The first dozen years of the band it was more like a chiefdom. I was the parent taking care of everything. As time has gone on there's things I got tired of doing, and which were draining me creatively. That is where the trust part kicks in.

Working with and coordinating our respective agents, plus dealing with venues, became a frustration that drove me mad. Such as we would pack a club, but at the end of the night the owner would say, "You did okay." What do you mean we did okay? We sold out the house, which is better than okay. They'd tell us things like they let 50 people in for free or cut the number down via some unexpected unspoken manipulation. Therefore, we weren't getting as big of a cut as we thought and we couldn't take credit for having a full house. "That wasn't part of the deal" was a phrase I said a lot. It was better than my old "this is not worth it" mantra, but the headache often felt the same. I would get so angry at times. Its a lousy way to end an otherwise good night, or its a great way to go over the line if the night already had problems.

For my own sanity I handed the job of tour manager over to my drummer Paul. I put my trust in his hands and Paul has been nothing short of amazing. He doesn't seem to let it all get him angry like it did to me. He can deal with the bickering agents, as well as the crazy venues. There's a language people in those roles speak that I really can't do, or even convincingly fake. I'm always an outsider in those negotiations and they know it. Its a brutal language. Listening to them I think they're going to beat the shit out of each other the way they treat and talk to each other. Then after what I thought was going to be a fight, they'll pat each other on the back like old friends or it was just a game. Yet, Paul can do it. He can dive into a pool of piranhas and come with the prize in hand. This is where trusting folks, and letting folks shine in places I really can't go, has really helped Kashmir.

A couple years ago I made a major change with Kashmir that nobody liked, the band nor my agent, until they saw my logic prove itself. I cut our number of shows in half.

We're getting older and its a bigger strain to go out, on top of the constant conflicts with our respective home and work lives and other bands. I decided I wanted to play less, which would lighten our physical strain and create less conflicts, but make equal or more money. Nobody was going to lose anything, while likely gaining time and money. I also wanted to be more selective in what gigs we chose. I didn't want to play anywhere, but with gigs that would be worthwhile experiences.

This was quite a reversal from the early days of Kashmir where we were chugging out a hundred shows a year. At one point I even tried to make Kashmir my full-time job. The wisdom of Little Steven's advice for having a back-up plan hadn't quite kicked in completely yet. I told my employer that I was quitting and becoming a full-time musician. He was cool about it and wished me luck, likely keeping his opinions to himself on the foolishness of my endeavor. There was a lot of conflicts with venues and balancing everyone's schedules, let alone bringing home a steady and doable income. A misstep or problem could domino and ruin multiple gigs, not to mention cutting into our income. While there's no holiday pay or sick leave available. No work means no pay, and gigs are one night things with no second chances. Obviously, it didn't work out in the end.

Yet, while I did go back to having a day job to ease the financial stresses, I still pushed myself with Kashmir longer than I probably should have. Living the rock star life is a dream come true for many of us. Making the rock star life function properly can be more like a nightmare. Rock stars rarely honestly talk about the daily grind that has broken up so many bands and ruined so many families. I found myself burning the candle at both ends. Trying to keep everything balanced could either be described as a constant hustle or an endless juggling game. Some might suggest its more like a house of cards.

I'd work my day job and then do the weekend warrior thing where I was driving off to a gig nearly every weekend. On top of that was periodic rehearsals and general band business. While so much of the time is spent on the road, preparing for a gig, and dealing with venues and agents. The show itself is but a small part of a musician's work. I run into a lot of people who think rock musicians are all druggies, but when you have to set-up and tear down and drive countless hours you don't have time for alcohol or drugs. Actually, the only thing you have time for is sleep and that is often interrupted and never enough. Its nearly impossible to have a life, let alone a dating relationship. One can only do this schedule for so long before the body suffers. If the body suffers than the performance suffers. The fun aspect goes out the window long before that, as the band becomes a job you can never go home from. At 25 or 35 its one thing to do a heavy schedule and maybe not be in the best physical shape, but did I want to blow my health before I got to 50. For what result?

I actually had some throat problems in 2019 that might have been caused by poor singing technique on top off too many shows on top of each other. I would go to hit a note and nothing would come out. It's a little scary going to a doctor wondering why no sound is coming out. The Covid-19 lockdown for a few months in 2020 actually helped me rest in important ways and greatly heal my voice. I managed to get back those missing notes and some of the range that I lost. I also started working with my falsetto to compensate. Over the lockdown I managed to feel a texture in my voice I hadn't felt in awhile.

The move from the clubs to the theaters was important change to grow the band, but now it was time for a change that would sustain the band better. I can't sing numerous times a week anymore, like in the Naked City and Avant Garde days, and maintain a good quality. I likely wrecked my voice those days more than I care to remember, but I was young and could fake it in the little clubs. I can't fake it anymore. I also don't want to. I'm in the shadow of the gods and when all is said and done, what am I doing? I'm in a tribute band. We're never going to get signed and make an album. Our goal is only about doing the best shows we can. As the body gets older its important to be aware that lots of gigs, on top of the traveling, on top of the paperwork, on top of the day job, on top of a home life, truly does become a house of cards. Working smarter than harder became my new game plan.

I've evolved so much. I went from a 21 year old with an insane libido who was distracted by everything around him, to a hard working professional who doesn't party and has a second non-music based income. I've got a wife who I like to be home with, versus partying till the break of dawn. The music business is not a stagnant process that never changes. It changes, while you change. There's no way to stay in and survive in this business without constantly growing and learning.

For those that might see me as a fuddy-duddy old man with odd bits of advice and a boring approach, the proof speaks for itself. Here I am in my 50's Kashmir is going as strong as ever, while my career might be better than ever. While Felix is older than me and has more energy than some of the teenage wannabe rock stars that I see. There's also still things I'm looking to achieve with the band. Spring and Fall are the big times for us due to the festival scene, but my goal is finding gigs in Florida and the south during the winter months. It would also be nice to expand our crew, which would ease some of the physical labor. Undoubtedly, I plan to be doing this for many more years. All of us do.

14

THE SONG REMAINS THE SAME

> *My peer group were writing substantial pieces of social commentary and I was wallowing along the Welsh borders thinking about Gollum.*
> ~ Robert Plant

In our set we do mostly the popular songs with a few lesser known ones for the die-hards. The anniversary of Zeppelin's first two albums was 2019, so we picked out some things from those two albums to do special. They did some great blues on those early albums that are fun to do.

Of course, we can never not do 'Stairway To Heaven'. One time we did not play it and several people complained that we sucked. We also cannot mess it up. If we do the whole night is a disaster. One time Andy messed up. He told me his imitation Jimmy Page jacket got caught on the guitar strings. I got mad at him after the show. He didn't think it was a big deal, but it very much is. We can mess up everything else but that song, cause everybody knows it by heart. If they know nothing else by Led Zeppelin they know 'Stairway To Heaven.'

'Babe, I'm Gonna Leave You' is a favorite of mine to do. Its just very bluesy and I like their blues stuff. 'In My Time Of Dying' is another great one, as Robert is just all over the place. Its vocally amazing and challenging and feels great to do it. 'Whole Lotta Love' is the song where we interact with the audience. We do it as a medley with 'Communication Breakdown.' It's fun. If we haven't won a crowd with that medley then we likely won't.

There are some songs we can't pull off. 'Trampled Under Foot' is one song that likely won't be heard anytime soon from us. This is my fault. Its the lyrics. I can't explain it, but I just can't remember those lyrics. Its about sex via car innuendos. I can't get into it no matter how hard I try.

Led Zeppelin had a wide variety of styles and it can be a challenge to get a song just right. 'Achilles Last Stand' is one of those. That song is like twenty minutes. We spent over a month working on it in rehearsals, but we couldn't get it to sound exactly right. We played it live once. Everybody went to get drinks. We took it out of the set immediately. The audience had voiced their opinion.

We learn the songs on our own and work out the logistics when we come together. Andy likes to pull out the fake books to get down all the exact notes that Jimmy played. Felix and Paul will do Jones and Bonham, but also put themselves in it. Though, if the sound isn't right or we're not all on the same page, I've been known to say we're not doing it right.

I've been asked if I listen to Zeppelin every day. Not deliberately, but sometimes I'll hear them on the radio or something will happen that is related to them, so I end up running into them some way seemingly every day. I don't own every Zeppelin album, nor do I track down bootlegs. I have their self-titled 1990 box set. My favorite albums are the debut and <u>Physical Graffiti</u>. I think Plant's voice is the strongest on those. I've read that the later one is also Plant's favorite. The <u>BBC Recordings</u> has been really valuable for me. Robert has so many nuances in those early live recordings. I like to find those parts not on the studio albums and put them into my performance. The <u>No Quarter</u> reunion special has also been a good resource. We do that version of 'Gallows Pole'. <u>How The West Was Won</u> has also been good for watching Robert's physical performance.

Of course, myself and the band can have everything planned out for the best possible performance, but things still happen that are unpredictable. In the early days of in-ear monitors they would shut down or create weird distracting noises. I've seen Paul's bass drum pedal fall off. I've thrown out my voice. Andy's guitar cable got loose, touching the floor and blowing all the monitors. Of course, we keep our cool like the professional troopers we are. Truthfully, sometimes we don't even know what's going on until after the fact.

There's also sometimes problems with people. I had a sound man who thought it was the 1980's where everything should be big. He'd pump the volume on every show. We have a lot of older folks who come to the shows, while sometimes we're in venues that are more intimate and better suited for acoustic shows. Its not necessary to pump the volume like we're in an arena. Complaints kept coming our way of people leaving as it was too loud, but my guy was like a chef who believed his recipe was perfect. I eventually replaced him with David since he wouldn't change his approach.

My agent wanted us to make a small promo video that would be a collage of scenes from our live show. We decided to film an actual theater gig for an authentic experience. We put up $4000 for a three camera set-up that would be our own Spinal Tap moment. Everybody loves that movie, but nobody wants it to be real, yet so many of us have seen how real it can sadly be. First, our van broke down on the way to New York from New Hampshire. We had to quickly rent another van and just made it with only an hour to set-up and soundcheck.

During Andy's guitar solo we sometimes had a friend come out dressed as the Hermit, the hunchbacked monk with an old lantern as seen in a painting inside the <u>Led Zeppelin IV</u> album. He would be pushed off stage in a fight with Andy's violin bow. With fog and lasers the scene is very mystical. Its reminiscent of the scene in the Led Zeppelin movie <u>The Song Remains The Same</u> where during a guitar solo Jimmy is shown climbing a mountain to reach the Hermit. We thought this would be cool for our promo.

We always set-up our own fog and lasers, but the theater crew said they had their own equipment. With the hour countdown that was in our favor. Andy starts his solo. The Hermit comes out. No fog or lasers to be seen. From the side of the stage I was literally jumping up and down trying to get the light guy's attention to turn on the effects. This was not mystical, but like a guy in a cheap Halloween costume fighting someone with a bow, or I had someone describe it to me as something from Alice Cooper's live show. I was so agitated that I hit a metal door backstage that fell forward and almost hit me. For more money could we have gotten our own mini-Stonehedge?

We later did another video, but we used a different company and put down $10,000. We were going to re-record the solo with the Hermit. We even had a new laser costing us $3000. I have a belief if something works we shouldn't mess with it. Of course, its also natural to want to try new things. The video crew suggested putting the laser up above the stage for a change and Andy thought that would be cool. He goes into the solo. The Hermit comes out. The fog rolls in. Thank you! The laser goes on. Success! Yet, it can't be seen. The crew had hung it improperly and it was focused on the ceiling. Andy soon faded behind the fog with nothing to see but accidental reflections on his guitar. The Hermit is nothing more than a ghost. While my hopes that this would be a successful video shoot also became ghosts.

As for other problems, festivals constantly battle the weather. Shows often get canceled or re-scheduled. We played once in Nashville. There was a really bad tornado going through. I'd just bought this Ford Ranger which we put the trailer on. Paul drove it to Nashville, while I flew, as we were coming from different places. He drove right through the tornado and got pelted with hail. Imagine a BB gun shooting off a thousand rounds. That's what the truck and trailer looked like. It was pretty disheartening to see. Paul is actually lucky he made it.

This night's trials and tribulations didn't stop with the weather. The club had one side with a dance club, with its non-stop pounding beat, and then we were on the other side. Our dressing room was in the middle. When we were done performing we got off stage to find a line going into our dressing room. Much to our sudden shock, that's where the restroom was. People were standing in line for the restroom waiting, talking, drinking. Right next to our stuff, that we thought was secure. They should have told us this was not a secure room. Let alone, were we supposed to get changed in front of everyone, or wait in the back of the restroom line?

Paul went off to deal with the money. Come to find out they were only giving us half. While he was gone I was looking for my jacket. With the line of people that had been going in and out of the restroom since we took to the stage I went crazy. I freaked out and started screaming as someone had obviously stolen my expensive jacket. Come to find out, while they really should have warned us the dressing room wasn't secure, we figured out I left the jacket in a restaurant. I was embarrassed. We never played at this venue again. My agent still rides me over this.

Sometimes Paul seems to be a magnet for tough situations, such as with problematic venues. Its not his fault, he just seems to be the unintentional victim for when something wild will happen, pelting hail aside. Kashmir went to Canada for some shows and we decided to use dry ice. Paul goes to cross the border crossing and everything is fine, until the border agents see smoke coming out of a cooler in the truck. There was Paul explaining in his thick stereotypical New York City accent how the storage of dry ice gives off smoke naturally.

There's also some strange things that have happened. Early on when the band was still playing an array of venues, we were booked to play at what I thought was going to be a hockey conference. It was more like a gathering of 1500 rough and tough members of a New Jersey biker gang. I told the band to keep to themselves and absolutely do not say we're friends with some potentially rival New York gangs. Two masochist clowns showed up. One would let anyone staple anywhere on his bald head for fifty bucks. "Do you want to?" No. "Do you want a demonstration?" I didn't even want to think about it. After the show he came back around and stapled to his head were three 50 dollar bills. He was actually very friendly and started complaining to us about how he had bad headaches. Really, dude? That's odd. I wonder why that happens?

There's been some bigger stuff that has happened of a more serious nature. In the clubs everything can be seen from the stage. I'll see these women dancing at the front of the stage and some stranger stalker guys will come up to them. I can see in the women's faces their shock as suddenly they have a dancing partner. They don't know what to do and in a crowd are often unable to quickly get out of the way. In the early days I would call the guys out to back off. I had a few guys get mad at me. One even tried pulling my hair cause he thought it was a wig.

One time Kashmir was playing a bar in Boston and there was ice all over the floor. This couple were really drunk. The woman fell and split her head open. She was unconscious for a bit with blood coming out. Nobody noticed. Her boyfriend eventually picked her up and was holding her as he rocked out to the music. He was so drunk he was completely oblivious to her injury and the fact she was essentially passed out. I saw this and didn't know what to do. Did anyone else see her? Was I imagining it? Nobody did, but I wasn't. Eventually we stopped the song and I called out for a doctor. Afterwards the club owner yelled at me, "You shouldn't have done that!" There was a woman who might have died tonight and I saved her life, but the owner was royally pissed. I took my money and said, "I'm gonna go now, cause you're an asshole."

There are also issues on the business end of things that crop up. When Time Of Dying became Kashmir I did a lot of research on the internet looking up all the other Led Zeppelin tribute bands. I wanted to find a name nobody else had, or at least was no longer being used. I didn't want to use Time Of Dying anymore as this was going to be a different entity with new members and a revamped sound. I didn't want people coming for Time Of Dying and finding themselves hearing a different band. That wouldn't be good for our future reputation.

After all my efforts to stake out my own claim in the world of Zeppelin tribute bands we're not the only Kashmir. Though, the other group formed after us. Every year I go through it with their founding guitarist. Could he not have found a different name? I think he saw us when we came to their area, so I believe he knew about us when he chose the name of tribute band. In the end, I often can do nothing but joke that the difference is we all have our real hair while they wear wigs. That hides my continual frustration. It is common to see people confuse the two bands, such as posters for them will feature our photos. I just throw up my hands. At least when I come across a website that shows a photo of us labeled as the actual Led Zeppelin I can chuckle. This is just frustrating.

The other Kashmir does a different show than us, so I'm not in competition with them. I've never tried to compete with anyone in any of my musical outings. My Kashmir has a different set-list, a different feeling in our show and a different sound. Their guitarist is focused on reproducing things exactly, while my Kashmir is looser in our interpretation and that's fine with us. Their website says that they're not trying to improve the music to put attention on themselves. I'm not sure if that's a dig on us or just tributes bands in general, but given they took our name I think it might mean he didn't like the way we played. They also do an acoustic thing where they have a cellist and violinist on stage, so we very much have different shows and there's no reason to compete.

I should have trademarked our name early on. If I gave any advice to a new band, aside from having a back-up financial plan, that would be it. I keep adding things to our name to differentiate our two groups, but they are paying attention to us as much as I pay attention to them. I called us Kashmir: The Ultimate Led Zeppelin Experience. Soon enough they were Kashmir: The Ultimate Led Zeppelin Experience. Then we were Kashmir: The Led Zeppelin Show, but I soon saw on their website that they were Kashmir: The Led Zeppelin Show. Currently we use Kashmir: The Live Led Zeppelin Show and they are Kashmir: The Led Zeppelin Show. Calling them a thorn in my side is an understatement.

Stepping back to look at the big picture I don't have a problem with their existence. I wish them the best. I don't have a problem with any Led Zeppelin tribute band. Not in the least. There's countless Zeppelin tributes that have come and gone over the decades of various looks and sounds and levels of authentic reproduction, ranging from cover bands to imitative tribute bands to non-rock interpretive groups. I learn from watching my fellow Zeppelin interpreters, like when I was inspired to do theaters from what I saw other Zeppelin tribute bands do. I see what works and doesn't work from what other bands do, so its good that there's many of us trying new things.

The problem is all about branding. From my research I found that none of the touring Led Zeppelin tribute bands shared the same name. A second band named Kashmir essentially means we really can't tour where they have. Luckily, they stay fairly close to home compared to us, but a few States in a certain area are now essentially cut off for us. If we go there people will see us thinking its them. They'll be expecting one show, but we'll be giving them something else. Even if they enjoy themselves seeing us, there will likely be folks wanting their money back since its a completely different band, even if it is the same songs.

I've explained this to my bandmates over the years, but they think I'm making a big deal out of nothing. They don't get it. It takes looking at the situation from a business point of view, not an artistic one. If someone sees the other Kashmir and goes away disappointed, and later see an advertisement for us, they might think its the same band who they don't want to see again. They might even tell their friends not so see us, on the mistaken assumption of our identity. This goes vice-versa, as someone might not like us and thus not want to see the other Kashmir. I no more wish bad reviews on them as I do on us. Its a brand thing, not a Zeppelin or tribute band thing. There's room for both us, if we had different names. This is one of those little dilemmas that haunt me. This goes in the same place in the brain which that desires to see the publishing royalties from World XXI. The place where bad dreams hang out.

For anyone who hears this complaint and thinks my bandmates are in the right and I really am making a big deal out of nothing, I actually speak from experience. When we formed Naked City there was another band in New York City also called Naked City. Formed in 1988 this was an experimental rock/fusion outfit formed by famed sax player John Zorn as a workshop to push the limits of improvisation across the musical spectrum. It included jazz guitarist Bill Frisell and briefly vocalist Mike Patton of the metal band Faith No More. It still is remembered to this day with ten albums to its name. We figured our Naked City, that was strictly rock and part of a different music scene, wouldn't be in conflict. We were wrong. They had a reputation coming out the door, which we ran into countless times to our detriment. I remember we played Montreal and half the audience thought they were coming to see John Zorn. We didn't go over well, to say the least. Had we ever been signed we would have been forced to immediately change our name. Making a poor choice with a name can be a haunting situation.

Being in a tribute band is interesting, as it is a world unto itself. Kashmir has brought a whole new education to my life as a musician.

All of us in tribute bands do what we do because we love our respective band and the music. Though, some famous bands openly don't like people imitating them and have actually clamped down on what tribute bands can name themselves, how they promote their shows and what they can do on stage. I think most are supportive. Some bands actually endorse different tribute bands with a stamp of approval, while some members of the real bands have joined on stage their tribute band cousin and vice versa.

We're actually helping the bands we imitate. We're doing live tour support for the real bands who aren't out touring.

People watch us and then buy their albums and singles. I've had numerous people compliment us by saying afterwards, "I never knew Zeppelin played that song. I really liked it. I went and bought the album." Some skeptics think that if fans see a tribute act then they won't go to the real thing when it comes to town. I heard of one band that went on tour in Europe and banned all tribute groups from playing during that time to not hurt sales. It was a move that actually didn't go over well with the bands and fans that had kept this group, at that pointed disbanded, selling in Europe after sales had faded in America. It was a back-handed compliment recognizing that the tribute bands were actually successfully promoting the real band. I find fans will see both if they can, as they want to hear the music and be a part of the experience as much as possible. Also, dedicated fans are notorious concert goers. I once knew of a woman who had seen Styx over 100 times, even mentioning them in books she wrote. At this rate it seems highly unlikely she'll see a tribute and and then stop seeing Styx. Further, we pay fees to ASCAP every year to play these songs, so the band is making money on our shows. They make more money the more we get out and gig. Who doesn't want what is essentially free money coming from some band in the middle of nowhere trying to be them?

15

STAIRWAY TO HEAVEN

I could no longer hide behind the veneer of being a rock star, the only thing left for me was to be real. ~ Ian Astbury

Its ironic that I would come to sing my sister's favorite band, yet I didn't like them as a boy. Christine would continue to love Zeppelin as an adult.

As kids, she would play the same song over and over and over. It would drive me crazy. I couldn't get into Zeppelin and she couldn't get into the New Wave I liked. I used to get into fights with her over this. It was a vicious childish stalemate. Due to life changes, we actually had a falling out for many years.

Yet, here I am today having heard the songs more than she ever did in all her repeated plays. Time Of Dying and Kashmir reunited us in a special way and brought everything full circle. Kashmir brought us closer than we ever had been growing up. She loved coming to see me and always glowed with excitement when I brought her backstage to hang out with the guys.

People like to claim music is magical, but in our case reuniting via Led Zeppelin was beyond special. I mention her coming to see us in the past tense, as she doesn't anymore. I lost her in 2008.

Kashmir was performing in Maryland. We'd had dinner and it was feeling like it was going to be a good show as we got ready to go on. I got a phone call from my mother. Christine was hit by a car. I was in disbelief. I called the hospital and the doctor said to get there immediately. Yet, the show must go on. I performed the first set, but choked up. We told the venue management what was going on and ended the show prematurely.

The guys took care of closing down as Andy hustled me into a car and drove to Jersey as fast as he could. She was brain dead. She was hit while walking not far from the house. It

was a hit and run. The driver was never traced. I had just been on the phone with her the day before. Today I have a well worn tie-dyed Zeppelin t-shirt of hers that she wore all the time.
    The collapse of Naked City was rough. World XXI had been devastating. This didn't even compare.

    It was the worst year of my life. The year before Christine died our grandmother had died. Then I found myself getting a divorce. The stress and commitment of being in a band can kill a relationship very quickly, let alone exasperate any other problems the relationship might have. Seeing her go was hard.
    I lost my grandmother and my wife, and as everything comes in threes, I then lost my day job. I was still living in the house I'd lived in married, surrounded by memories, and attempting to survive on Kashmir. It was frustrating and mind-numbing.
    My mom ended up moving in. My parents had gotten divorced. Dad was re-married and still in Florida. I took care of her as she had COPD from smoking. While I didn't have a day job, Kashmir was taking me on the road for so many hours and so often that it became a difficult to properly take care of her being essentially alone and from a distance. Christine came to help. She was amazing and I would have fallen apart without her. Then I lost her. My mother ended up moving into a nursing home.
    In 2008 Kashmir was in upstate New York. It was a really good show and afterwards we went to a karaoke bar. I got hammered. I rarely do that and don't know what got into me. I remember a magician was there and we had a great night. Of course, I was out of it and collapsed into bed. When I got up my phone was blowing up with messages. Mom had died. Had I not been drunk I might have seen the messages earlier or heard the phone ring. I haven't drank like that since.

    I was so distraught at what life had handed me I just wanted to get away. For a long time I was mad at life. I was blaming everybody for everything and anything. I was also heartbroken and feeling someone ungrounded. Four women had left my life in one year.
    It took over a year to get my life back together and feeling somewhat normal. In late 2008 my family had a

celebration for my grandmother, mother and sister, as we placed their ashes in the Gulf of Mexico.

    The only thing that kept me going during this time was Kashmir. The guys were supportive, while the music took me out of my head. Rehearsing and performing kept me sane. The music of Led Zeppelin and the guys were my lifeline.

16

WHAT IS &
WHAT SHOULD NEVER BE

The rooms you create in — whether the lights are on or off, what you're going through in your personal life — all of this comes into the room.
~ Ian Astbury

    Kashmir has been my art and my therapy, my teacher and my family. There's no autopilot and there's always new things I'm learning and new things the band is trying. I really love what I do, but there's been times when those around me haven't loved it quite as much.

    In order to sing the blues you need to bleed, I believe Ian Astbury once said. Playing in a band can be incredibly hard on personal and professional relationships. My first wife was a casualty of it, but she wasn't the first nor the last to willingly step out of the picture. My girlfriends all enjoyed the music, but supporting it was a different matter. The band is my life, not theirs. Yet, it ends up becoming theirs and that didn't always work for them. I've seen relationships fall apart for nearly everyone in my circle due to playing in a band.

    A good example is when a gig gets moved due to bad weather. Now maybe I have to be on the road on a day I was planning to spend with my girlfriend for some personal time. My schedule is thrown off and so is hers. Maybe that personal time is not easy to re-schedule with our respective activities. Whoever I'm married to or dating suddenly finds her life is being planned around my gigs as much as my life is. Except one of us gets to perform on stage, while the other is now home unexpectedly alone.

    I've made a commitment to Kashmir that might be hard for an outsider to understand. The best comparison might be a marriage, or maybe someone who owns their own business and can't just take a day off on a whim. I wouldn't ask someone to give up their own business, while I'm not giving up Kashmir. I come to every relationship with baggage in the form of a rock band. My baggage is a handful of grown men who twiddle knobs, pluck strings, pound things, handle money and more. I've been doing music all my life, which means sometimes I have to leave someone I had hopes for on a personal level because it conflicts with the band. Its not easy. It hurts. Doing what I do doesn't make me immune to the call of the heart or able to deal with break-ups any easier.

Or, there's situations such as when I have to drive all night after the show and will have three hours of sleep before hauling myself to work. Coming home after a day at work I'm likely exhausted, so that disrupts the time I have at home or the time I might be spending with someone. I'm falling asleep while someone else wants to do something. It can sometimes be very stressful to get through the day with some level of normalcy. To drag someone into this with me is not a very fair deal. Many musicians fall into drugs and alcohol to drown the frustrations as the struggle between band and home life can sometimes seem insurmountable.

For some the conflict between the band and a relationship is solvable by letting the band end. For them the band is replaceable, but not the person. Some have even left the industry completely as it took away too much time from family obligations. This hasn't been my case, but sometimes I can see it coming in others. An early drummer in Kashmir, Brian, always struggled to find a girlfriend. Then his luck changed and they fell madly in love, eventually getting married and starting a family. The relationship became his priority over the band. He made a choice to not jeopardize what he'd long been looking for. Of course, I don't blame him and totally understood. I'm happy for him.

This is not to mention women I've dated who like the music, actually can deal with the schedule, but don't like being on the other side of the rock world. Jealousy is something that comes up often with the partners of musicians. I'm singing romantic songs on stage with my shirt open. Women are in the audience dancing, drinking and having a good time. They'll try to pick me up after a show. I take it as complimentary, as it means I've done my job for the night. I always politely turn them away, as I'm faithful. I also know that it might be Robert Plant they are seeing and not Jean Violet. Once had a girlfriend who couldn't deal with that aspect of the performance. She got very jealous seeing the girls gaze and flock to me.

Being in a band also effects professional relationships. I've had my agent offer me gigs in the very near future, but I couldn't take the time off from work at such short notice. I also don't have unlimited time I can take off. Some bosses are willing to make allowances, others no so much.

Being a weekend warrior, which is a huge population of musicians including some famous bands long past their commercial heyday, requires a master level of juggling. Trying to make the band, the crew, my wife, my job, not to mention the venue and my agent, all happy can require a lot of sacrifices. On many occasions they all were happy, while I ended up making myself miserable.

People think we get on stage and life is all candy, but they don't understand how much of a sacrifice us professional musicians make sometimes. In the early years of Kashmir when we were doing 100 shows a year there was barely a week where we didn't have at least two shows. While these are commitments that can't be easily broken if I feel like I just want a night in. While venues are famous for threatening lawsuits and imposing fines on bands that want to pull out of a gig.

I have friends, and relatives, who I don't see or talk to for long stretches of time. Its not personal. Yet, surprisingly, sometimes someone will get upset at me and think I'm deliberately avoiding them. "What's your problem?" I've been accosted with too many times. If I'm doing a hundred shows a year plus working a day job, plus a relationship and other normal life responsibilities, the truth is I'm not avoiding anyone. Actually, the truth is I'm likely barely finding time to sleep.

In 2018 I got married a second time. Marilyn and I were together about five years at that point, so she'd seen my life enough to know what baggage I brought with me. I don't have kids or a horrible ex or a secret criminal past. I have a band. Kids or the other options might be easier sometimes. Marilyn is an amazing trooper to be able to take in my baggage. I'm blessed to have her.

When we met I was still living in New Jersey and she was in Maryland. We thus started our life separated by time apart and physical distance. That may have been a long term key to our success. She's very independent and has her own full time job and life, and none of that stopped when we moved in together. She does come to a gig when she can. I likely spend about five hours a week on band related stuff, outside of gigs and rehearsals and being on the road, but I try to not let the band suck away all my time and take me away from her. We might have been lucky and started our relationship on the right foot for long term success, but that doesn't mean I take it or her for granted.

Marilyn has so much patience and gives me the support I need and want. Her support actually drives me and helps me through the difficult and tiring moments. One part of the equation is the quasi-anxiety that can come when the band is not on the road for stretches of time, like during our slower season or the coronavirus lockdown of 2020. My music and my art are my things, so when I'm not doing one or the other for extended amounts of time I can get a little ungrounded. Marilyn is my rock in those times.

When I was a youth and ripping it up on stage I was like every guy looking to party, have fun and get laid. In my 30's I realized there had to be more to the life of a musician than that. Since my 40's I've learned its not about being on stage looking for a passionate encounter, but putting passion into my performance for this grand experience in a room full of strangers. I want to communicate with my audience in subtle ways I didn't when I was young. With my Marilyn supporting me its so much easier to do that.

Every time I sing Zeppelin's 'Thank You', with just Andy strumming the chords next to me to open the song, I think of Marilyn. In my mind I'm singing to the face I saw in the very first picture she ever gave me of herself. The song regularly gets a standing ovation because they can feel the passion. I'm not really Robert Plant in that moment. I'm Jean Violet who is singing thank you to the person who gives me the life I want and need.

17

ACHILLES LAST STAND

Time is so valuable. I don't put anything out that I don't have 110% passion for. Otherwise I've got plenty of other things I could do with my life.
~ Robert Plant

Around 2016 I unexpectedly returned to doing some original music when an opportunity presented itself. Kashmir had a gig in Charlotte, North Carolina and opening was a Black Crowes tribute band. They were pretty good. The guitarist and I ended up hanging out that night.

He later contacted me and said, "I have this Deep Purple meets Led Zeppelin thing, all originals, would you be interested?" I was interested and I liked his playing. He started sending me some music. I actually didn't feel any drive to do anything original again. That was a part of my past and I was happy with Kashmir, but I liked the music he was creating. That's the thing that really drew me in. Even Marilyn thought this was something I could do really good with.

Thus was born Violet Sunn Armada. He had the music written and most of the lyrics, except for one song I contributed in memory of my sister and mom, called 'Promised Land.'

That being said, we were going in 50/50. I know he did a lot of work before he reached out to me, but I brought to the table years of experience, industry connections, my marketing and art experience, and I'd build the website. Yet, as we kept going on and the music got fleshed out with a drummer, bassist and keyboardist there was a struggle that developed. It was essentially his project, but he sold it to me as a partnership. It was slowly starting to not feel like a partnership.

In this business, in order to succeed, one has to be willing to compromise. It may not be the first choice of action, but, if someone is footing the bill they may ask for certain things. "No" can't be the answer, as the other party can just as easily respond by withdrawing their support, money and enough to collapse the project. While, to walk into a room and tell people, maybe strangers, how things are going to be and that's the way it is will often achieve the same dead end results. A lack of compromise can kill the relationships and the creativity pretty fast. I saw that happen with Hiro and Yasumi with World XXI. The result was lots of enemies and an album that needed to be re-recorded and re-mixed. I wasn't going to suffer through that again, let alone trying to save the Titanic.

I don't know if he realized what he was doing to Violet Sunn Armada's potential for success. I was pretty sure what I was feeling likely would be felt by others and hurt us in the end. Though, in his defense, he might not have dealt with others the way he was working with me, but there were other fault lines appearing that fed into my leeriness. We started to talk publishing and he wanted to put it all under his name. It began to feel too much like World XXI. I also began to feel like he thought I was stupid, and thus could pull something over on me. I know how things work in this business all too well. I haven't been successful by being stupid. Naively hopeful, yes, but not stupid.

Another argument was over the name. He wanted to call it just Armada. There's tons of bands named Armada. If we got a label to sign us there would be lawyers from those bands coming after us day one. Branding is important. He didn't get it, just like some of my bandmates didn't understand my issues with the other Kashmir, even though I'd seen it firsthand with Naked City and John Zorn's Naked City. For awhile we were SoulFinger before settling on Violet Sunn Armada.

When one person tries to control everything that's how things don't get done as people start to shut down. This time I was the one who shut down, I saw the signs this time around and was adding them up. I wasn't itching to do original music again so badly that I was willing to put myself into a miserable situation.

He found another singer and re-recorded the vocals for an independent EP release. While he named the group Armada, of course. We're still friends. I wish him all the best, but from my experience I just didn't see me being able to do what I needed to do in that project. I've got to enjoy what I'm doing, and people we bring in to it should enjoy it. Nobody wants to be a part of a toxic environment. While if Violet Sunn Armada was toxic than it might spill over into Kashmir. I'm not going to harm my bread and butter.

Before I left, we did end up putting out online in 2018 a nine song EP online, <u>Mind's Eye</u>. That is also the name of one of the songs. Its no longer available, though the songs can be heard on the studio's website as part of their portfolio. The song to my family is the only one I asked not to be shared by the studio, as its too personal to float it out as part of a dead project. <u>Mind's Eye</u> has a very Zeppelin bluesy guitar vibe with complimentary Deep Purple organ and rhythms, but modern flashy guitar solos. Its very retro and good stuff, experience aside. The other good thing that came out of the project was the keyboardist became Kashmir's soundman.

I wouldn't mind doing some original music again, but it has to be with the right people and right circumstances. More importantly, we're actually working together or the working relationship is clear and stays the course. If I was driven to make original music then I'd probably go out there and make it happen. I'm not, I was fine letting the sun set on Violet Sunn Armada.

PROMISED LAND

Never thought that it could happen
Never thought it'd end like this
Just had a conversation laughing
Now I'm drowning
Drowning in my tears

Well it seems like yesterday
When I got that dreaded call
In my hotel getting ready before showtime
When it all went straight to hell

(chorus)
Now I know there will come a day
When I see you once again
We will dance and sing with angels
Walking through the promised land

In the sweet sunlight sweet sun

Sometimes life has only questions
With no answers to be found
I keep searching for a reason to understand
Something good could be so wrong

Mama I can hear you crying
I can feel your broken heart
How the pain led you to dying
All I ask is that you meet me
When my time has come

(chorus)
But I know there will come a day
When I see you once again
We will dance and sing with angels
Walking with you in the promised
The promised land

(refrain)
Its hard to stop the tears from falling
Its hard to heal this broken heart

But I know there will come a day
When I see you
See you once again
We will dance and sing with angels
Walking in
We will stand
Walking in the promised land
Walking in the promised land
When I see you
We will dance and sing with angels
I see you in the promised land

18

YOUR TIME IS GONNA COME

I hope people coming to the concerts take away a sense of love and optimism, connection and communion.
~ Ian Astbury

Once upon a time I wanted to be this rock star. That guy on MTV and on the radio. Well, I did, sorta. I'm not on MTV, nor on the radio, but I did figure out a way to make music, do what I love, pay the bills and have a fulfilling life. I may not quite be the rock star I dreamed of, but I'm in the shadow of rock star gods, in more ways than one. I get to play one and play on the same stages with them, hang out with them, and sometimes be treated as one of them, and I had my time signed to a label and touring with them on two continents. I'm happy with the ways things turned out.

There's so many bands that don't make it, so to spend a couple decades with a tribute band playing some of the greatest songs in rock history is a real pleasure. Its a long way to the top. Its not an easy path. I once heard the phrase, "You have a better chance of winning a lottery than being Guns N' Roses." That is so real and not even an exaggeration. That is reality.

Yet, there is one more story to be told. A very important one. That being the moment that I knew I'd made it. A bucket list moment, for lack of a better term. There's many ways of judging success, including fame and fortune and fan accolades and a million twitter followers, but when one's peers take notice that means something was done right.

Coldplay's frontman Chris Martin was throwing a huge 30th birthday bash for his actress girlfriend Dakota Johnson. Her favorite band is Led Zeppelin. Zeppelin is even the name of her dog. For a stupid amount of money he had Kashmir come out to his place in Malibu Beach to play a private gig as a birthday gift in October 2019. The event was covered by England's newspaper The Daily Mail, including a photo of us performing, with the headline "Inside Dakota Johnson's 30th birthday: Actress wore a plunging white jumpsuit as she treated her A-list guests to a silent disco, a rock star performance and a dog-shaped cake." In attendance was Gwyneth Paltrow, Miley Cyrus, Kate Hudson, Robert Downey, Jr. and Kenny G.

After the performance I asked Chris, "How did you find and choose Kashmir?" He told me, "I asked some of my friends who was the best Led Zeppelin tribute out there and they told me it was Kashmir." He spent some time on youtube and came to agree with them.

That was the moment I knew I'd made it and that my time had come. Bucket list achieved.

THE END

... FOR NOW

Us boys of Avant Garde looking animal-like. This is actually a rock band publicity shot and not a promotion for a hairspray company. I'm seated center with (left to right) Matt Tichon, Donny Weingartner, Kurt Foltz, Mark Pertocelli.

*Naked City looking dark and moody.
This image was featured in an article about
up-and-coming rock bands in Metallix magazine.
Left to right: Randy Liez, Michael Angelo, me, Brian Kreis,
Kurt Foltz.*

Naked City with me center looking very Jim Morrison-esque. Left to right: Brian Kreis, Kurt Foltz, me, Buzz, Michael Angelo.

Naked City mentioned in New Jersey's <u>East Coast Rocker</u>, now known as <u>The Aquarian Weekly</u>.

THE ONLY WEEKLY MUSIC NEWSPAPER IN THE USA

East Coast ROCKER

PLEASE RECYCLE THIS NEWSPAPER

NAKED CITY

If LA Guns are the "LA Vampires" then Naked City are New York's version. Not to be confused with John Zorn's Naked City, this hard rock quintet take pride, and maybe a little well-deserved conceit at being one of New York City's best live rock bands. Naked City were officially formed about two years ago in the Lower East Side by frontman Jean Violet and bassist Kurt Foltz. Both originally from Pittsburgh, the two decided to relocate and conquer N.Y.C. together. After a bit of convincing, seasoned guitarist Michael Angelo (his real name) joined. To complement his blues roots, the almost complete Naked City found guitarist Brian Kreis. And where would Naked City be without drummer Randy Lyes, who when not playing the city's best rock clubs, seems to be there anyway showing off over $6,000 worth of tattoos.

Not restricting themselves to New York City, Naked City did a three-week stint up in Canada, thanks to the Canadian band, Sven Gali. Naked City currently dominate the N.Y.C. scene playing the Cat Club and the Limelight frequently. In the past, Naked City have played Woody's and Sanctuary in addition to all the trendy clubs. The band have received rave reviews from the *Musician's Exchange*, Canada's *Winnipeg Sun*; and even *Metalix* magazine.

As for tapes, Naked City's impressive demo features some of their best songs including "Magic Strikes At Midnight," "Hungry," and "Devil In Her Eyes." During the New Music Seminar, Naked City showcased for numerous labels at the Cat Club.

Naked City in their mystical element in the East Village. Left to right: Kurt, Brian, me, Michael, Buzz.

PRESENTED BY MOLSON CANADIAN

happy as a clam

WINNIPEG SUN   AUGUST 1990

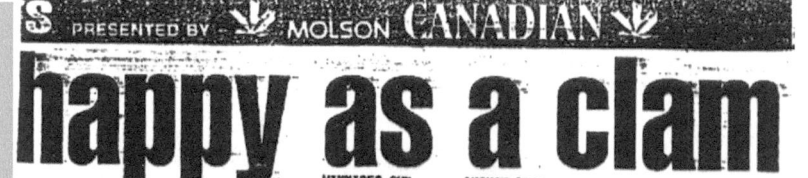

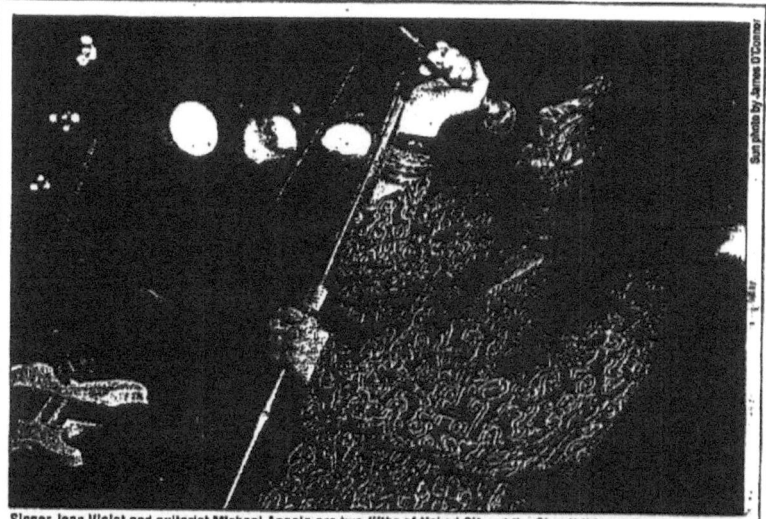

Singer Jean Violet and guitarist Michael Angelo are two-fifths of Naked City, at the Circuit this weekend.

PICK OF THE WEEK

There are thousands of bands in New York City. And Naked City is just one of them.

Which is why this quintet of hard-rockin', black-wearin' vampires has ventured up to the Great White North for a three-week tour.

"In New York we might only play six or seven times a month," says bassist Kurt Foltz. "And then it's just one 40-minute set of originals. Boom, you're done."

"So to come up here and to play six nights a week is just a great opportunity for us," pipes in singer Jean Violet. "It allows us to come out here and tighten up so that when we go back we'll just be smokin'."

Violet may be a little off-base there. His Naked City is already smokin'.

Playing a hybrid of original music that marries the sound of Nazareth, Motley Crue and Riot (a great NYC band from the early '80s) with the energy of speed-metal, the group is an incendiary device ready to explode.

All five play their guts out with an in-your-face aggression rarely seen in these parts. Violet's acrobatics and his menacing histrionics combine the attitude of Skid Row's Sebastian Bach with the energy of The Cult's Ian Astbury-wearing-Jim-Morrison's clothes.

And it's not surprising group with similar attitude, energy and music is responsible for bringing Naked City to Canada.

"You can blame Sven Gali," laughs Foltz. "We played with them on a bill at a New York club called the Limelight, and we liked each other and each other's music and they said, 'hey, you should come up and play'.

"So here we are, and we love it. This is a tour for us."

Naked City was formed just over a year ago in Manhattan by Violet and Foltz, who had been working together in Pittsburgh. They moved back to New York, bugged guitarist Michael Angelo (his real name) until he joined them, and guitarist Brian Kreis and drummer Randy Lyes hooked up shortly thereafter.

Rehearsing regularly the group developed its own tunes and managed to land gigs in the city's top metal clubs, so now its members have focussed their attention on landing a recording deal.

The "vampires" of Naked City featured in the *Winnipeg Sun*, with a picture of yours truly on stage at the now defunct Circuit.

World XXI's only album. The Japanese version has "XXI World XXI" typed in the center and a different color scheme. World XXI with (left to right) Dave Crigger, me, Hiro Kuretani, Mac Mizunuma.

*The second line-up of World XXI.
Left to right: Kurt Foltz, Bruce Edwards, me, Hiro.*

Me while touring America with World XXI.

A full page ad in <u>Metal Edge</u> magazine, October 1995, with the second line-up of World XXI.
Left to right: Hiro, me, Bruce, Kurt.

Time of Dying at Madison Square Garden.
Left to right: Aaron Brooks, Kurt Foltz, Jimi K. Bones,
Joe Chiofalo, me, and Brian McGee.
Kurt must get a nod for being a part of so much of my career,
as all these photos show.

Me backstage at Madison Square Garden with Time of Dying.

Here I am lost in time and space with Kashmir.

*I'm feeling the energy with Kashmir.
Kashmir looking very much the part with
(left to right) Felix Hanneman, me, Paul Cooper,
and Andy Urban.*

I'm getting into the zone with Kashmir.
With my right hand man Andy in his decorative
Jimmy Page outfit.

Here I am a happy man in the shadow of the gods.

Doing my golden god pose.

Me at a Kashmir soundcheck.

COLLECTORS EDITION
Rolling Stone

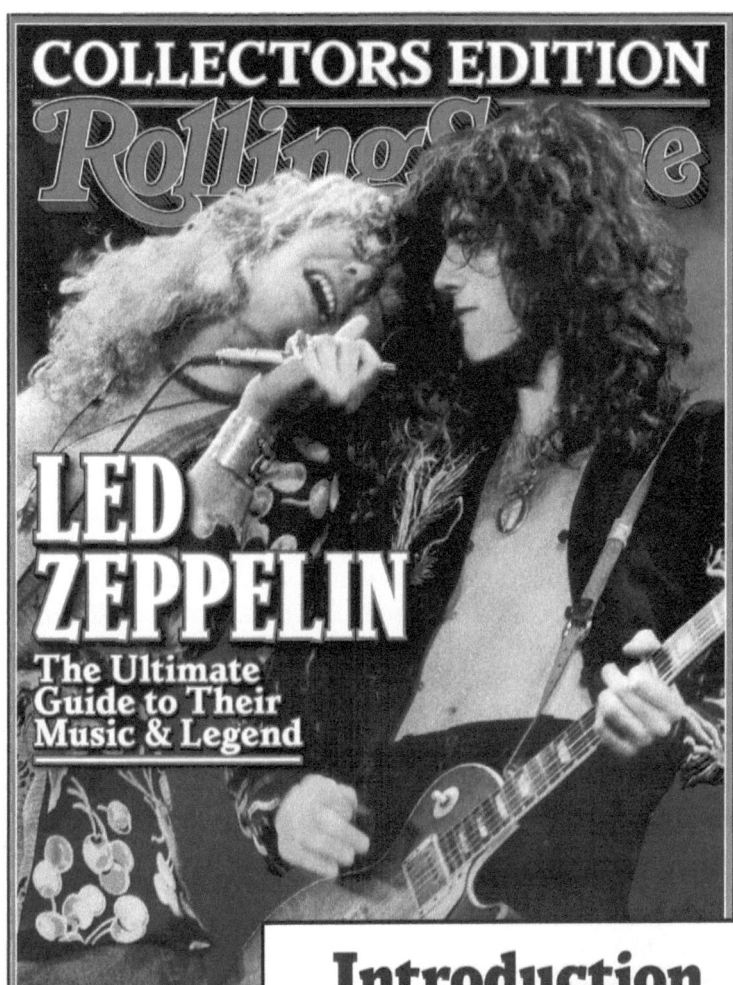

LED ZEPPELIN
The Ultimate Guide to Their Music & Legend

Introduction

MORE THAN THREE DECADES AFTER THE end of Led Zeppelin, they are everywhere. They've sold nearly 25 million albums since 1990 alone, and every night bands with names like Kashmir, No Quarter and Lez Zeppelin cover their songs in bars and clubs worldwide. This year, an ultrasquare Republican vice presidential candidate bragged about having them on his iPod, and in December they'll be honored by the black-tie crowd at the Kennedy Center for the Performing

Rolling Stone Collectors Edition on Led Zeppelin mentioning Kashmir on the first page of the lead article.

CO-AUTHOR'S AFTERWARD

CAROUSELAMBRA

Rarely does the story behind the story gets told. I believe the story behind this memoir provides a nice coda to Jean's bucket list. I don't know if I believe in fate, but I do like a good moment of coincidence.

For six years I'd been researching and writing a biography of a one-off '90's supergroup. I had published a handful of books, both non-fiction and prose, but for some reason this one always eluded finalizing even with a largely completed draft. It was like there was always something missing, but I could never quite figure out what it was. I'd write a bit, put it away for a year, pull it out to scribble or research something, put it away for another year, etc..

Having written the biographies of the hair metal band Danger Danger and Latin jazz pianist Irving Fields, along with editing two non-music related biographies, I decided it was time to finish my draft in the fall of 2020. Perhaps if I kept my focus from wandering then the missing piece would reveal itself. The only observable task outstanding was to make another attempt at finding a handful of musicians from the book for interviews.

One band mentioned in the book is World XXI. I'd been unable to track down Mac and Hiro, due to the language barrier and them largely leaving music as a full time career. I only knew Hiro had become a DJ after his time with Stephen Pearcy. I'd found Dave in 2018 via his posting some of World XXI on youtube. He'd referred me to his singer who was in the Led Zeppelin tribute band Kashmir, Jean Violet. I'd gone on Kashmir's website, but my focus faded once again and the draft was retired.

Two years later out it came and I decided to do a deeper hunt for Mac and Hiro. On facebook I found a guitarist with Mac's name. There was nothing about World XXI on the page, but I found a comment by a guy named Hiro Kuretani. Translating the Japanese didn't give any details to verify if I had found half the band, but this was too much of a coincidence.

Then I spotted another comment by a guy that looked like Robert Plant. It was the singer, which confirmed I'd found World XXI.

Given the language barrier I decided to first reach out to Jean first. I e-mailed him about my book, what I knew of his band and what I was looking for. He wrote back saying he was impressed I'd done my homework, and we could talk on the phone that weekend. I had no expectations. My book is a tribute and not a detailed history, so anything he shared would be welcomed.

He gave me a buzz and then happily detailed his past life and his career since. It helped that we had both had lived in New York City, so I knew of the people and places he referenced. After an hour, as we were winding down, he said he had long wanted to write his memoir. Was I interested? I don't know what moved him to ask, but that moment became life changing for both of us with the result being this memoir.

He outlined his thoughts for the next 30 minutes. By the time I went to bed a few hours later I had a complete chapter outline in my head with emotional highs and lows charted out. A few days later I sent him the outline and a proposal. The response was he was into it "110%". Our respective ladies also approved the new partnership, which is very important. In order to roll you have to have your rock.

I read so many music biographies its like an addiction. Far too many are cliched stories of sex, drugs, parties, with the music as an afterthought. It is almost as if the stars are told that their fans want lots of raunchy stories, yet perusing through music forums will show discussions of what went into the music is on the lips of most fans. We want to know the real people and how they created the music we love, not the fake tabloid persona. Somewhere in the middle is likely the best place, with a bit of the rock lifestyle alongside the art of crafting music. Also, most music biographies have no story. They are essentially a series of vignettes that don't lead anywhere other than the natural passage of time, outside of death or a climactic career changing event.

I didn't want to write a cliched rock memoir and neither did Jean. I'd already been dragged down that rocky road with a musician who publishers had turned away saying they wanted more about the band and less about the women. Like Jean's time with Armada Sunn Violet, I didn't want to repeat my past just for the sake of a new project. Jean and I also both wanted something a bit educational, like one musician offering advice to another but without getting preachy and arrogant. Essentially, paying forward the wisdom of Little Steven, Don, Jimi, mixed with Jean's own personal growth. While I wanted to write a story. I actually had in mind Ian Fleming's James Bond novels, which are famous for their cliffhanger chapter endings. I gave each chapter its own emotion in the writing process.

Our respective visions of what we wanted to do with a rock memoir seamlessly blended and it remained that way through the months the book was written. What makes our meeting more interesting is years earlier Jean had gone to a fortune teller of some sort who had said he should write the memoir he was dreaming of. He hadn't told her anything about his dream. I don't know if he ever proposed it to any other authors, but it obviously wasn't meant to be until our meeting.

I wrote at the beginning that I like coincidences. It is an ironic coincidence that I did not contact Jean when Dave told me about him. Ending this memoir with the birthday party was the obvious conclusion when Jean proposed the book to me. It brings a sense of conclusion to his story, which instantly had me hooked as a writer. Yet, when I talked to Dave this event was a year away. It thus feels like a coincidence my other book was never finished, almost like Jean and I were meant to connect but after his big gig. If one believes in a guiding hand of fate, than I was delaying not because of my lack of focus, but because Jean needed to achieve something to complete his story so we could write his story.

We can both honestly say we had mutual dreams come true with this memoir. We had a great time working together. Jean has even proposed a second book. Ironically, my six year biography is now going on seven years as Jean's adventures have inspired me. I've long wanted to write a novel, but could never find a story. Jean's life inspired me and now I have one novel outlined and another one half written. One of them features a tribute band. Not so much a coincidence this time.

~ Aaron Joy,
December 2020

CITATION CREDITS

1. hightimes.com/culture/high-times-greats-robert-plant (1991)
2. shorelocalnews.com/the-evolving-culture-of-the-cult-the-shore-local-interview-with-lead-singer-ian-astbury (2018)
3. billboard.com/articles/news/8238651/robert-plant-dan-rather-big-interview-clip (2018)
4. songfacts.com/blog/interviews/ian-astbury-of-the-cult (2012)
5. loudersound.com/features/robert-plant-interview-my-life-after-led-zeppelin (2020)
6. independent.co.uk/arts-entertainment/music/features/robertplant-interview-on-his-new-album-and-his-led-zeppelin-days-9683308.html (2014)
7. bravewords.com/news/the-cult-frontman-ian-astbury-for-me-the-idea-of-making-albums-is-dead (2009)
8. songfacts.com/blog/interviews/ian-astbury-of-the-cult (2012)
9. nationalpost.com/entertainment/ian-astbury-takes-dead-aim-at-critics-of-the-cult-on-choice-of-weapon (2012)
10. rollingstone.com/music/music-features/robert-plant-the-rolling-stone- interview-103788 (1988)
11. loudersound.com/features/robert-plant-interview-my-life-after-led-zeppelin (2020)
12. irishnews.com/arts/2016/02/26/new/meditation-is-where-its-at-says-ian-astbury-of-the-cult-427151 (2016)
13. shockwavemagazine.com/ian-astbury-the-cults-front-man-opens-up (2017)
14. iheart.com/content/2019-05-15-robert-plant-thinks-he-ruined-a-few-led-zeppelin-songs-with-his-lyrics (2019)
15. nationalpost.com/entertainment/ian-astbury-takes-dead-aim-at-critics-of-the-cult-on-choice-of-weapon (2012)
16. archives.sfweekly.com/shookdown/2015/11/17/we-talked-to-ian-astbury-of-the-cult-about-budweiser-reincarnation-and-ok-computer (2015)
17. uncut.co.uk/features/all-the-old-gods-are-long-gone-but-still-an-interview-with-robert-plant-4474 (2014)
18. therockpit.net/2019/interview-ian-astbury-billy-duffy-the-cult (2019)